BLAKE'S Grammar Guide

for primary students

Del Merrick

PASCAL PRESS

Blake's Grammar Guide

Reprinted 2010 twice, 2011, 2012

ISBN: 978 1 92136 750 2

Published by Pascal Press
PO Box 250
Glebe NSW 2037
www.pascalpress.com.au
contact@pascalpress.com.au

Author: Del Merrick
Publisher: Lynn Dickinson
Edited by Shelley Barons & Kerry Davies
Design and illustration by Janice Bowles

Printed by Green Giant Press

CONTENTS

CONTENTS continued...

AUSTRALIAN CURRICULUM CORRELATIONS - YEAR 3

LANGUAGE	ELABORATIONS	ACELA	PAGE
Language for interaction Examine how evaluative language can be varied to be more or less forceful	★ exploring how modal verbs, for example 'must', 'might',' or 'could' indicate degrees of certainty, command or obligation ★ distinguishing how choice of adverbs, nouns and verbs present different evaluations of characters in texts	1477	26, 42, 76 3, 22, 40, 69-72, 77
Text structure and organisation Understand how different types of texts vary in use of language choices, depending on their function and purpose, for example tense, mood, and types of sentences Know there are lower and upper case letters	★ becoming familiar with typical structural stages and language features of various types of text, for example narratives, procedures, reports, reviews and expositions	1478	30-33, 37-38, 49-51, 54-55, 74-75
Understand that paragraphs are a key organisational feature of written texts	★ noticing how longer texts are organised into paragraphs, each beginning with a topic sentence/paragraph opener which predicts how the paragraph will develop and is then elaborated in various ways	1479	59
Know that word contractions are a feature of informal language and that apostrophes of contraction are used to signal missing letters	★ recognising both grammatically accurate and inaccurate usage of the apostrophe in everyday texts such as signs in the community and newspaper advertisements	1480	28-29
Expressing and developing ideas Understand that a clause is a unit ofmeaning usually containing a subject and a verb and that these need to be in agreement	★ knowing that a clause is basically a group of words that contains a verb ★ knowing that, in terms of meaning, a basic clause represents: what is happening; who or what is participating, and the surrounding circumstances	1481	63, 74 35, 52-53, 56
Understand that verbs represent different processes (doing, thinking, saying, and relating) and that these processes areanchored in time through tense	★ identifying different types of verbs and the way they add meaning to a sentence ★ exploring action and saying verbs in narrative texts to show how they give information about what characters do and say ★ exploring the use of sensing verbs and how they allow readers to know what characters think and feel ★ exploring the use of relating verbs in constructing definitions and descriptions ★ learning how time is represented through the tense of a verb and other structural, language and visual features	1482	24 71 24, 71 24 30-33
Learn extended and technical vocabulary and ways of expressing opinion including modal verbs and adverbs	★ exploring examples of language which demonstrate a range of feelings and positions, and building a vocabulary to express judgments about characters or events, acknowledging that language and judgments might differ depending on the cultural context	1484	42, 76-77
LITERATURE		**ACELT**	
Examining literature Discuss how language is used to describe the settings in texts, and explore how the settings shape the events and influence the mood of the narrative	★ identifying and discussing the use of descriptive adjectives ('in the middle of a vast, bare plain') to establish setting and atmosphere ('the castle loomed dark and forbidding') and to draw readers into events that follow ★ discussing the language used to describe the traits of characters in stories, their actions and motivations: 'Claire was so lonely; she desperately wanted a pet and she was afraid she would do anything, just anything, to have one to care for'	1599	11 72
LITERACY		**ACELY**	
Creating Texts Plan, draft and publish imaginative, informative and persuasive texts demonstrating increasing control over text structures and language features and selecting print,and multimodal elements appropriate to the audience and purpose	★ using appropriate simple, compound and complex sentences to express and combine ideas	1682	54-55, 74

AUSTRALIAN CURRICULUM CORRELATIONS - YEAR 4

LANGUAGE	ELABORATIONS	ACELA	PAGE
Text structure and organisation Understand how texts are made cohesive through the use of linking devices including pronoun reference and text connectives	★ knowing how authors construct texts that are cohesive and coherent through the use of: pronouns that link back to something previously mentioned; determiners (for example 'this', 'that', 'these', 'those', 'the', 'his', 'their'); text connectives that create links between sentences (for example 'however', 'therefore', 'nevertheless', 'in addition', 'by contrast', 'in summary')	1491	10, 21, 60-61, 79-80
	★ identifying how a topic is described throughout a text by tracking noun groups and pronouns		9, 21, 81
	★ describing how texts connectives link sections of a text providing sequences through time, for example 'firstly', 'then', 'next', and 'finally'		60
Expressing and developing ideas Understand that the meaning of sentences can be enriched through the use of expanded noun and verb groups and phrases	★ creating richer, more specific descriptions through the use of noun groups (for example in narrative texts, 'Their very old Siamese cat'; in reports, 'Its extremely high mountain ranges'	1493	9, 70, 73
Investigate how quoted (direct) and reported (indirect) speech work in different types of text	★ investigating examples of quoted (direct) speech ('He said, "I'll go to the park today"') and reported (indirect) speech ('He told me he was going to the park today') and comparing similarities and differences	1494	57-58, 62, 66
Understand how adverbials (adverbs and prepositional phrases) work in different ways to provide circumstantial details about an activity	★ investigating in texts how adverbial phrases and clauses can add significance to an action, for example 'more desperately', 'he rose quietly and gingerly moved'	1495	47, 56, 64-65, 73
LITERACY		**ACELY**	
Creating Texts Plan, draft and publish imaginative, informative and persuasive texts demonstrating increasing control over text structures and language features and selecting print,and multimodal elements appropriate to the audience and purpose	★ using appropriate simple, compound and complex sentences to express and combine ideas	1694	54-55, 63, 67, 74
	★ using grammatical features effectively including different types of verbs, adverbials and noun groups for lengthier descriptions		9, 24, 40-44, 47, 70-71

AUSTRALIAN CURRICULUM CORRELATIONS - YEAR 5

LANGUAGE	ELABORATIONS	ACELA	PAGE
Language for interaction Understand that patterns of language interaction vary across social contexts and types of texts and that they help to signal social roles and relationships	★ identifying ways in which cultures differ in making and responding to common requests, for example periods of silence, degrees of formality	1501	75-77
Text structure and organisation Understand that the starting point of a sentence gives prominence to the message in the text and allows for prediction of how the text will unfold	★ observing how writers use the beginning of a sentence to signal to the reader how the text is developing (for example 'Snakes are reptiles. They have scales and no legs. Many snakes are poisonous. However, in Australia they are protected')	1505	59, 78
Understand how possession is signalled through apostrophes and how to use apostrophes of possession for common and proper nouns	★ examining how conventions of punctuation are used in written and digitally composed lists and learning that in Standard Australian English it is not necessary to add another 's' to the end of a plural noun to indicate possession ('Connors' house'/ 'my parents'car')	1506	6
Expressing and developing ideas Understand the difference between main and subordinate clauses and how these can be combined to create complex sentences through subordinating conjunctions to develop and expand ideas	★ knowing that the function of complex sentences is to make connections between ideas, such as: to provide a reason (for example 'He jumped up because the bell rang.'); to state a purpose (for example 'She raced home in order to confront her brother.'); to express a condition (for example 'It will break if you push it.'); to make a concession (for example 'She went to work even though she was not feeling well.'); to link two ideas in terms of various time relations (for example 'Nero fiddled while Rome burned.')	1507	63-66, 74-75
Understand how noun and adjective groups can be expanded in a variety of ways to provide a fuller description of the person, thing or idea	★ learning how to expand a description by combining a related set of nouns and adjectives – 'Two old brown cattle dogs sat on the ruined front veranda of the deserted house'	1508	9, 46, 70, 72-73
LITERATURE		**ACELT**	
Examining literature Recognise that ideas in literary texts can be conveyed from different viewpoints, which can lead to different kinds of interpretations and responses	★ identifying the narrative voice (the person or entity through whom the audience experiences the story) in a literary work, discussing the impact of first person narration on empathy and engagement	1610	18, 58
LITERACY		**ACELY**	
Creating Texts Plan, draft and publish imaginative, informative and persuasive print and multimodal texts, choosing text structures, language features, images and sound appropriate to purpose and audience	★ using appropriate grammatical features, including more complex sentences and relevant verb tense, pronoun reference, adverbials and noun groups for lengthier descriptions ★ using paragraphs to present and sequence a text	1704	9, 30-33, 40, 47, 55, 63-66 70-71, 73-74 59

AUSTRALIAN CURRICULUM CORRELATIONS - YEAR 6

LANGUAGE	ELABORATIONS	ACELA	PAGE
Text structure and organisation Understand that cohesive links can be made in texts by omitting or replacing words	★ noting how writers often leave out words that have already been mentioned (eg'Tina ate three apples and Simon ate two. [apples]') ★ noting how writers often substitute a general word for a more specific word already mentioned, thus creating a cohesive link between the words (eg 'Look at those apples. Can I have one?') ★ recognising how cohesion can be developed through repeating key words or by using synonyms or antonyms	1520	80 79-80 14, 81
Understand the uses of commas to separate clauses	★ identifying different uses of commas in texts	1521	62
Expressing and developing ideas Investigate how clauses can be combined in a variety of ways to elaborate, extend or explain ideas	★ knowing that a complex sentence typically consists of an independent clause and a dependent clause connected by a subordinating conjunction (eg 'because', 'when', 'after', 'if', 'while', 'although'). Note: Dependent clauses of time, purpose, reason, concession, condition and so on are referred to as 'adverbial clauses' ★ knowing that the function of complex sentences is to make connections between ideas, such as: to provide a reason (eg 'He jumped up because the bell rang'); to state a purpose (for example 'She raced home in order to confront her brother'); to express a condition (eg 'It will break if you push it'); to make a concession (eg 'She went to work even though she was not feeling well'); to link two ideas in terms of various time relations (eg 'Nero fiddled while Rome burned')	1522	60-61, 63, 80 65, 75
Understand how ideas can be expanded and sharpened through careful choice of verbs, elaborated tenses and a range of adverbials	★ knowing that verbs often represent actions and that the choice of more expressive verbs makes an action more vivid (eg 'She ate her lunch' compared to 'She gobbled up her lunch') ★ knowing that adverbials can provide important details about an action (eg 'At nine o'clock the buzzer rang loudly through the school.') ★ knowing the difference between the simple present tense (eg 'Pandas eat bamboo.') and the simple past tense (eg 'She replied.') ★ knowing that the simple present tense is typically used to talk about actions that happen regularly in the present (eg 'He watches TV every night.') or that represent 'timeless' actions, as in information reports (eg 'Bears hibernate in winter.') ★ knowing that there are various ways in English to refer to future time (eg 'She will call you tomorrow'; 'I am going to the movies tomorrow'; 'Tomorrow I leave for Hobart')	1523	22 40-44, 47, 65, 71-72 30-31 30 30, 32
LITERATURE		**ACELT**	
Responding to literature Identify and explain how choices in language, for example modality, emphasis, repetition and metaphor, influence personal response to different texts	★ noting how degrees of possibility are opened up through the use of modal auxiliaries (eg 'It may be a solution'; 'It could be a solution.') as well as through other resources such as adverbs (eg 'It's possibly/probably/certainly a solution.'); adjectives (eg 'It's a possible/probable/certain solution'); and nouns (eg 'It's a possibility/probability.')	1615	26, 42, 76
LITERACY		**ACELY**	
Interacting with others Participate in and contribute to discussions, clarifying and interrogating ideas, developing and supporting arguments, sharing and evaluating information, experiences and opinions	★ recognising that closed questions ask for precise responses while open questions prompt a speaker to provide more information	1709	75
Creating Texts Plan, draft and publish imaginative, informative and persuasive texts, choosing and experimenting with text structures, language features, images and digital resources appropriate to purpose and audience	★ using rhetorical devices, images, surprise techniques and juxtaposition of people and ideas and modal verbs and modal auxiliaries to enhance the persuasive nature of a text, recognising and exploiting audience susceptibilities	1714	39, 42, 76
Reread and edit students' own and others' work using agreed criteria and explaining editing choices	★ editing for coherence, sequence, effective choice of vocabulary, opening devices, dialogue and description, humour and pathos, as appropriate to the task and audience	1715 65, 79	11, 46, 56-57,

HOW TO USE THIS BOOK

This book has been written as an easy grammar reference for students from middle primary upwards. Each of the major sections of the book contains simple concise definitions of grammatical terms as well as an easily understood example of the usage. For example:

> **Proper nouns**
>
> **Proper nouns** give people, places, objects and events their given or special names.
>
> For example: Jane, Mars, Olympic Games, Sydney, Uluru
>
> Proper nouns are easily recognised because they always begin with a capital letter.

Most of the definitions are followed by a quick 'TRY THIS' quiz to allow students to consolidate and test their new knowledge. Answers to the 'TRY THIS' sections are provided at the back of the book.

Blake's Grammar Guide also contains a detailed index for locating the specific term you need more information about, as well as a comprehensive glossary of terms for quick reference.

There is also an extensive section on Functional grammar, which explores and explains the experiential, interpersonal and textual function of language.

ABOUT THE AUTHOR

Del Merrick is an experienced teacher currently working for Education Queensland as a Support Teacher, Learning Difficulties. She has taught in many primary schools, both nationally and internationally, and has undertaken various educator positions including Key Teacher, English; Further Literacy In-service Project Consultant; 'First Steps' Tutor; Education Adviser; Literacy and Key Learning Area Regional Coordinator, English.

Del has worked extensively with educators in both the state and non-state systems, providing strong leadership and professional expertise while guiding and supporting changed classroom methodology and improved literacy practices. She is the author of many educational materials, including the best-selling *Targeting Grammar* series, and has designed an extensive range of professional development workshops and resource materials for educators. Her personal interests include a passion for poetry and music.

Introduction

Every language has an underlying structure called its grammar – an arrangement of words into 'pieces of language' that we can all recognise and understand. This grammar drives the way we select and arrange our words so that we are able to communicate and connect with each other easily.

Because we learn to speak through listening, mimicking, experimenting and getting feedback, we have an almost unconscious and lasting knowledge of how our language works. We observe the ways in which language is constructed for different purposes; then we bend and shape it and hone our skills, until we are able to say exactly what we want to say every time we want to say it.

Reading requires knowledge of how written (and visual) language is represented. We need, for example, to understand that we read in meaningful chunks, called phrases and sentences, and we interpret the punctuation marks that guide us through the natural flow of expression. Our speaking vocabulary is enriched through exposure to the many texts we read (and view).

Writing requires us to apply our knowledge and understanding of grammar. We need to know how to build our text, sentence by sentence, paragraph by paragraph; and the devices we can use to tie it all together, so that readers can make sense of what we write. Writing also demands the added features of spelling and punctuation, format and presentation.

Words are the building blocks of all language. In English these words fall into different groups, with each group having a particular job to do. The main groups are: nouns, pronouns, verbs, adjectives, adverbs and prepositions. Knowledge of what words 'do' in a sentence also supports the spelling process. We understand how and why we must alter words to maintain the structures of our language. This book will give you an understanding of the **language** of grammar and guide you through its use.

Del Merrick

NOUNS

Common nouns name the everyday things in our world – people, places, objects and animals.

For example:
girl, actor, river, shop, computer, chair, goanna, possum, lake, pizza

Nouns name people, places, animals and objects

Number nouns

Nouns may be **singular** in number.
Singular nouns name ONE thing.
box train football flower match rose

Nouns may be **plural** in number.
Plural nouns name MORE THAN ONE thing.
boxes trains footballs flowers matches roses

To write regular plural nouns, we add **s** to the singular noun.

houses bells trees elephants rivers biscuits lemons boats

OR we add **es** to nouns that end in ch, sh, s, ss, x and some words ending in o.

benches wishes buses kisses foxes volcanoes potatoes

Irregular plural nouns are formed by changing the vowels or adding **en**.

foot feet
woman women
man men
child children

Make a list of ten common nouns that name things around you.

TRY THIS

Some nouns are both **singular** and **plural**.
sheep fish deer

Some nouns are **only plural**.
trousers scissors spectacles shears

Write the plural form of these words.

SINGULAR	PLURAL	SINGULAR	PLURAL	SINGULAR	PLURAL
plate		truck		child	
pencil		beach		sheep	
shoe		lunch		tooth	
book		snowman		violin	

Proper nouns

Proper nouns give people, places, objects and events their given or special names.

For example: Jane, Mars, Olympic Games, Sydney, K-mart, Uluru, Sunday, Christmas, April, Swan River, India

Proper nouns are easily recognised because they always begin with a capital letter.

Take this quick quiz. All answers are proper nouns. Each begins with a capital letter.

a city	a movie star	a shopping centre	a day
a river	a month	a special holiday	a country
a state of Australia	a book title	your sister or brother	a mountain
a desert	a newspaper	a magazine	a make of car
a nationality	a brand of coffee	a bridge	a song

Compound nouns

Compound nouns are made by joining two words together.

For example: snowflake, heartbeat, tablecloth, sandcastle, butterscotch, basketball

Some **compound words** are hyphenated words.
ice-cream forget-me-not line-out ping-pong mass-produce

With use over time, these words will eventually be spelt without the hyphen. *Today* and *tonight* were once hyphenated – *to-day* and *to-night*.

Write a minimum of 20 compound words, built from the words below. Words can be used more than once.

fire	river	line	farm	way	bush	water
place	head	bed	house	light	clothes	land
room	side	hill	life	under	time	top

Collective nouns

Collective nouns are names given to groups of animals, people or things.
For example: flock of birds, herd of cows, crowd of people, packet of biscuits

A collective noun means a single group even though there may be more than one member of the group. Therefore when a collective noun is the **subject**, it is followed by a singular verb.

A flock of birds *is flying* across the sky.
The team *is leaving* the dressing room.

Find the collective nouns in this text.

A crowd of people gathered along the seacoast. It waited patiently to photograph the pod of whales moving slowly northward. A shoal of fish and a school of porpoises swam by. A flock of birds screeched noisily overhead. After several hours a cheer went up. The pod of whales had finally arrived.

Possessive nouns

Possessive nouns show ownership.
An apostrophe is always used.

For example: Jack's horse; children's shoes; the teacher's book; Dad's beard; six hens' eggs; the cats' whiskers

Use 's for single owners.

Possessive nouns name the **single owners** of things.
Brenda's bucket   Jim's Akubra
the boy's dirty hands

Place the apostrophe after plural owners.

Possessive nouns name the **plural owners** of things.
zebras' stripes   dogs' bones
the girls' muddy clothes

TIP: Add an apostrophe to ANY noun that ends in s.
Add 's to a noun that DOES NOT end in s. (There are a few exceptions to this rule.)

Abstract nouns

Abstract nouns give names to the thoughts and feelings within our hearts and minds.

For example: love, hope, despair, gratitude, anger, joy, beauty, greed

You cannot see or touch abstract ideas – they exist in your thoughts and in your feelings.

Circle the nouns that name abstract ideas.

sorrow	porcupine	glamour	clarinet	chieftain
hope	anger	lantern	container	tolerance
happiness	laundry	despair	chalk	grief

Verbal nouns

Verbal nouns are words ending in **-ing** used as nouns. They show action but they also name something.

For example: Skiing is a winter sport. Shall we go bowling? Seeing is believing.

Verbal nouns are also called **gerunds**.

(See also Participles p.25)

Find the verbal nouns in this text.

Waiting for the storm to hit was scary. The wind started with a soft murmuring, which soon grew to a terrible roar. The constant screaming of the wind soon filled our ears and rattled the windows. Then there was the unmistakable cracking of branches being broken by the wind's fury. We watched as the fierce wind tore the roofing off the shed. The whistling and whining of the wind seemed to go on for hours. Gradually the wind died down to a low moan, followed by a deathly silence. The storm had finally passed.

Gender nouns

Gender nouns refer to either males (masculine) or females (feminine).

For example: boy (male) girl (female)
bull (male) cow (female)

Pair the nouns – masculine and feminine.

aunt	goose	stallion	king	gentlemen	ewe
ladies	princess	man	rooster	gander	prince
mare	woman	queen	uncle	ram	hen

Many gender nouns have a **common gender** – male or female.
author doctor poet instructor thief scientist

Many nouns are neither male nor female.
They are **neuter** in gender.
sun leaf book car planet rose house

Noun suffixes

Suffixes are syllables attached to the ends of words. Some suffixes form nouns.

For example: kindness, amazement, justice, intention, dancer, violinist, childhood

A number of suffixes are used to indicate people with particular jobs, roles or professions.

-er	-or	-ian	-ent	-ant
baker	sailor	electrician	student	dependant
dancer	actor	musician	client	merchant
teacher	doctor	guardian	recipient	assistant
-eur	**-ee**	**-eer**	**-ive**	**-ist**
amateur	employee	engineer	native	dentist
connoisseur	trustee	buccaneer	captive	soloist
restaurateur	refugee	musketeer	fugitive	optometrist

(For more about suffixes, see p.13)

Noun suffix: dancer

We can change other word forms to nouns by adding particular suffixes.

educate (verb) education (noun)
accurate (adjective) accuracy (noun)

Knowing how to change words, phrases and clauses to nouns can help us to write in very precise ways. This is especially useful in report writing.

The major problem is that the rivers are very polluted.

River pollution is now a major problem.

(For more about Nominalisation, see p.84)

Noun groups

A **noun group** is a group of words built around a noun. It often contains words that describe the **head** noun.

For example: a tiny, black spider; a squat, brown teapot; one chocolate and almond cake; long-awaited news; my straw hat

Noun group:
a squat, brown teapot

Noun groups are a major feature of our language. We are constantly composing text around them.

Noun groups are used to name the **participants** in text – the people, animals or objects that are involved in events. (See p.70)

Participants may be the **subject** or the **object** of a sentence. (See pp. 52,53)
My friend (subject) sent me a birthday card (object).
Roses (subject) grow in my garden.
You (subject) should taste this pumpkin soup (object)!

Noun groups are used in **preposition phrases**. (See pp. 45, 70)
Stir the soup in *the pot* on *the stove*.
He was speaking to *the crowd* before him.
The snake slithered over *the log* towards *the trough*.

What are the noun groups in these sentences?
I ordered a cheeseburger and a piece of apple pie.
A mean, sly fox was prowling around the farmer's henhouse.
During the night, rain fell gently on the rooftops and windowpanes.
A family of noisy magpies lives in a shady tree in our garden.
The class watched an interesting documentary about earthquakes.

Articles and nouns

There are three **articles** in English, which we often use to introduce a noun group. The articles are **a**, **an** and **the**.

For example: a tip truck, an apple, the daily newspaper

The article **a** is **indefinite**. We use it when we are talking about something or someone non-specific or not familiar.

a bag of potatoes   a television set   a library book

The article **an** is also **indefinite**, and does the same work as **a**. It is used before a word beginning with a vowel, or an unsounded **h**.

an ant   an egg   an old man   an opera   an hour
an overpowering smell

a and **an** are only used when talking about singular nouns.

The article **the** is a **definite article**. We use it to talk about something or someone specific or familiar. It is used to introduce both singular and plural nouns.

the boy by the door   the house on the hill   the last page

the eggs in the nest   the apples on the tree

the is always used when it introduces something or someone known by everyone.

the sun   the moon   the night   the morning   the afternoon   the prime minister

When we introduce a person or thing (noun) for the first time, we usually begin the noun group with **a**. As we talk more about this person or thing, we use **the**.

Would you like a biscuit? Thank you. I'll have the one with red sprinkles.

Underline the articles in this passage.

Once there was a wild horse. It was snowy white with a long flowing mane. The horse could sometimes be seen in the late afternoon, just before the sun went down. Then it would disappear into a dark, rocky cave.

One day, an adventurer who had been walking in the hills, was looking for a cave where he might sleep for the night. Behind a large shelf of rock, he found a small cave. It was the cave where the white horse lived.

ADJECTIVES

Adjectives give meaning and life to nouns

Adjectives describe nouns.
They work with the noun to give clear pictures of people, places and things.

For example: strong athlete; exciting news; shaggy, black dog; tiny, round beads

Descriptive adjectives

Adjectives give life and personality to all the people and things we speak and write about. Speakers and writers create images of people and things partly through their choice of adjectives. These adjectives are often chosen specifically to give a positive or a negative view of people, places, events and objects. (See p.72)

Cinderella is pretty, poor, hardworking, alone and isolated. (We are 'invited' to feel sorry for her.) The step-sisters are mean, ugly, lazy and bossy. (We are 'invited', not only to dislike them, but to align ourselves with the unfortunate and unhappy Cinderella.)

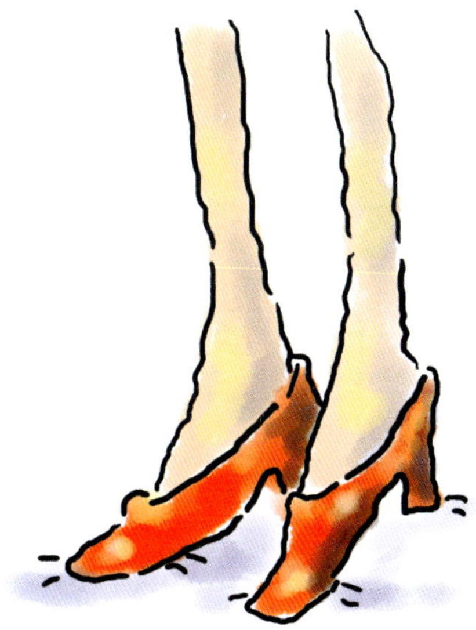

Descriptive adjective: red shoes

Descriptive adjectives give nouns:

- colour – red shoes, rosy cheeks, green forest, pale face
- sound – deafening roar; quiet voice; hushed whisper
- shape – round pot; circular track; oval table
- size – large meal; tiny ants; short rope
- feeling – angry mob; sad boy; hungry animals
- qualities – menacing smile; fascinating story; lazy Jack

Adjectives can be placed **before** the nouns they describe,

I like crunchy, red apples.
We went for a long, tiring walk.

OR, **after** the nouns they describe.

The apples are red and crunchy.
Our walk was long and tiring.

Find the adjectives that describe the underlined nouns.
Sports Day finally arrived. It was a sunny, cold day. I put on my new, red T-shirt and black shorts and slipped into my trusty, old sneakers with the fluoro laces. I had a light breakfast and hurried off to school on my silver bike.
We gathered on the school oval in our teams. I was the fastest runner in my class, but just before the finishing line, I stumbled. All the other runners ran past and I crossed the line in last place. I tried not to cry, but it was a great disappointment.

Number adjectives

Adjectives show number.

For example: ten geese, five marbles, sixth person, first place

The adjective can show a **definite** number.
two eyes eight legs last night
seventh place

The adjective can show an **indefinite** number.
some marbles a few days many seeds
several months most people

Verbal adjectives

Verbal adjectives have both a verb and an adjective function. (See p.26)

For example: a walking stick; falling rocks; a deafening roar; scented roses; a puzzled look; a dazed expression

Verbal adjectives end in **-ing**, **-d**, **-ed**, **-n**, **-en**.
For example: swimming pool, ground pepper, painted wall, torn clothes, hidden cave

Find the verbal adjectives in these sentences.
I like stewed apple and baked custard.
I have amazing photos of the cheering crowd.
He had fried eggs and bacon on a toasted bun.
We heard exciting news about the missing climbers.
I listened to the howling wind with growing concern.

Adjective suffixes

Suffixes are syllables attached to the ends of words. Some suffixes form adjectives.

For example: funny, helpful, careless, famous, comfortable, attractive, foolish

The suffixes **-ful** and **-less** create words that are opposite in meaning.
These words are called **antonyms**. (See p.14)

helpful	helpless	careful	careless
colourful	colourless	useful	useless
restful	restless	powerful	powerless

We can change other word forms to adjectives by adding particular suffixes.
depend (verb) dependable (adjective)
sun (noun) sunny (adjective)
drink (verb) drinkable (adjective)

Add suffixes to complete these sentences.
Choose from -able, -al or -ish.
Grandad is sitting in his comfort_____ armchair.
The weather bureau forecast coast_____ showers.
She is such an agree_____ person.
That was a fool___ thing to do.
A diary is a record of your person____ life.

(For more about suffixes, see p.8)

Antonyms

Because the work of adjectives is to describe nouns, it is possible to use them in ways that give opposing views of people and things.
These adjectives are called **antonyms**.

For example: short/tall person; fresh/stale cake; sweet/sour oranges; rough/smooth road; dull/bright day

Here is a list of some everyday antonyms.

hot/cold	fast/slow	big/little	large/small
new/old	wide/narrow	long/short	old/young
wet/dry	clean/dirty	right/left	rough/smooth

Some antonyms are formed by adding prefixes to the adjective. The prefixes, **un**, **in**, **im**, **il** and **ir** are the most commonly used.

Add the prefixes given. Read the words.

un	in	im	il
happy	dependent	possible	legal
usual	formal	probable	literate
truthful	visible	patient	legible
clean	appropriate	mature	logical

Adjectives of degree

Adjectives often compare the qualities of people and things.
These are **adjectives of degree.**

For example:
a big house, a bigger house, the biggest house
a long rope, a longer rope, the longest rope

There are three degrees:

- **positive** – describes a quality of a person or thing.
  Will is a tall boy.
- **comparative** – makes a comparison between the qualities of two people or things.
  Jack is taller than Will.
- **superlative** – shows the highest degree of difference compared to all others.
  Hamish is the tallest boy in our class.

Positive degree:
sad

comparative degree:
sadder

superlative degree:
saddest

Sometimes we add **–er** and **–est** to show comparative and superlative degrees.

old older oldest　　high higher highest
dry drier driest　　sticky, stickier, stickiest
sad sadder saddest　　fine finer finest

Sometimes we use **more** and **most** before the adjective. This occurs when the adjective already has a suffix.

famous	more famous	most famous
attractive	more attractive	most attractive

Sometimes the words themselves are changed.

good better best　　bad worse worst
many more most

Complete the adjectives of degree correctly.

- Evan is a fast__ runner than Jackson.
- Death Valley is one of the hot___ places on Earth.
- I am good at chess, but Helen is much ________.
- Kim was the _____ helpful person in the library.
- That was the long_____ movie I have ever seen!

TRY THIS

Similes

Adjectives are used in **similes**. Similes are short phrases that point out a likeness between two things.

For example: as light as a feather;
as cold as ice; as white as snow; as soft as silk

Similes provide vivid word pictures of people and things. They often exaggerate the truth and add colour and interest to our language, both spoken and written.

Find the similes in these sentences.

Dad told me to be as quiet as a mouse.

Last night, the sky was as black as ink.

The road lay before us, straight as an arrow.

He stood in front of the principal, shaking like jelly.

She looks as pretty as a picture in her new yellow dress.

TRY THIS

PRONOUNS

Pronouns are used instead of nouns in speaking and writing.
Personal pronouns replace the names of people and things.

For example: Matthew is a strong diver.
He won a gold medal.
Stephanie is a great swimmer. She broke two world records.

Pronouns replace nouns in speaking and writing

Personal pronouns

Personal pronouns can be **singular** or **plural**.
They can be **male**, **female** or **neutral**.

SINGULAR	PLURAL
I, me	we, us
you	you
he, him	they, them
she, her	they, them
it	they, them

Personal pronouns replace the names of people and things.

The pronouns I, he, she, it, we and they are used in **subject** position. (See pp.35,52,70)

This is a parrot. It has a hooked beak.

Jack and I go swimming.

He likes pasta.

She likes pepperoni.

We like peanuts and popcorn.

They like peas, potatoes and pumpkin.

The pronouns me, him, her, it, us and them are used in object position. (See pp.36, 53)

Jo gave me a banana.
Jo gave him an apple.
Jo gave her a peach.
Jo gave it some sunflower seeds.
Jo gave us a watermelon.
Jo gave them a bag of oranges.

Person

FIRST PERSON:
the speaker – I, we

SECOND PERSON:
the one spoken to – you

THIRD PERSON:
anyone or anything else – he, she, it, they

Pronouns fall into three categories:
first person pronouns
second person pronouns
third person pronouns

These categories distinguish between:

- the speaker – **first person** (I, me, my, mine, we, us, our, ours)
- the person being spoken to – **second person** (you, your, yours)
- anyone or anything else – **third person** (he, his, him, she, her, hers, it, its, they, them, their, theirs)

A writer uses **first person** pronouns to tell a story from a personal point of view. This is most common in diaries and personal recounts.
A writer uses **second person** pronouns when his characters speak directly to each other or when the writer speaks to the reader.
A writer uses **third person** pronouns to tell a story about other people and events. This is most common in story telling.

Are these statements made from a first person, second person or third person point of view?

Possums are nocturnal animals. They hunt for their food at night.

You should collect your things and hurry home before you get wet.

I joined my team on the field for our final soccer game.

We went to the train station to see our friends off.

They will have a game of handball after they have lunch.

Possessive pronouns

Like nouns, **possessive** pronouns show ownership.

For example: This book is hers.
Here is our house.
The children put on their hats. Tom ate his dinner.

Unlike nouns, pronouns do not require an apostrophe.
Compare:
This is Jane's book. (possessive noun) (See p.6)
This book is hers. (possessive pronoun)

POSSESSIVE (Singular)	POSSESSIVE (Plural)
my, mine	our, ours
yours	yours
his	their, theirs
her, hers	their, theirs
its	their, theirs

For example:

This is my book. It is mine.
This is your hat. It is yours.
This is his computer game. It is his.
This is her watch. It is hers.
These are our model planes. They are ours.
These are their marbles. They are theirs.

Interrogative pronouns

Pronouns are used to ask questions.
The interrogative pronouns are:
who, whom, what, which, whose.

Who is coming to the disco?
What would you like to eat?
Which hat is yours?
Whose house is this?
To whom did you speak?

Possessive pronoun: your hat

Demonstrative pronouns

Demonstrative pronouns refer to specific people and things. The pronouns are: **this**, **that**, **these**, **those**.

For example:
This is the way to the football stadium.
These are the photos I took in Europe.

Demonstrative pronouns are very often used in speech where the speakers are able to point to the things they are talking about, or they have a shared understanding about the context of their interaction.

Indefinite pronouns refer to people and things in a general way.

Indefinite pronouns

Indefinite pronouns refer to people and things in a general way.

For example: Has anybody seen my beach ball?
There are only a few left. Soon there will be none.

Indefinite pronouns include: any, all, anybody, anyone, each, everybody, everyone, everything, few, many, no-one, none, nothing, several, some, somebody, someone, something.

They is also indefinite when we make statements like, 'They say it's going to rain tomorrow'.

TRY THIS

Add an indefinite pronoun to complete the sentences.

Does ____________ know if Sally is coming to school today?
When he scored the winning goal, ___________ cheered.
It looked like rain, but _______ fell.
We're having pizza. Do you want ________?
I thought I saw ____________ at the window.

Reference

Pronouns refer backwards and forwards to people and things.
They 'tie' ideas together.

Jacob has four pet birds. He gives them seeds and water every day.

Pronouns usually refer backwards to a person or thing that has already been introduced. (See p.79)

The hikers, with backpacks on their backs, climbed steadily to the base camp of Mt Everest. The mountain towered above them. It looked much too steep for them to climb.

The plane took off in light rain. The passengers sat back in their seats for take-off, with their seat belts fastened. The plane was soon in the air. It climbed rapidly and within fifteen minutes, it was cruising at very high altitude. A flight steward walked down the aisle. She handed headphones or magazines to each passenger.

The plane was soon in the air. It climbed rapidly.

Add the missing pronouns.

Barbara Sox looked up when Peter entered the kitchen. ____ noticed the grease under _____ fingernails. ' ______ has been under that old car again,' Barbara thought. ______ frowned and went back to ______ sketching. Peter realised that if ______ wanted a cup of tea, ___ would have to get ____ himself!

VERBS

Verbs are the essential ingredient in any communication

Verbs consist of one or more words that tell us what is 'going on' in a sentence.

They are the essential ingredient in any communication.

For example: A snake is a reptile. Tanya is speaking to her mum. Dylan has pet mice. Birds fly. Jake bought some popcorn.

Verbs show the particular interactions and relationships between people, places, events and objects.

Verbs link ideas and give them meaning.

The children → **were reading / are writing / bought / like** → books.

Like adjectives, verbs give colour and interest to language. They create strong images of movement, action and behaviour so can be used to great effect, especially in descriptive writing and poetry.

Compare: 'The waves ran up on the sand and ran slowly back to sea'

and

'The waves thundered and crashed on the sand, then retreated slowly'.

Simple and compound verbs

A **simple verb** consists of one word.
The kookaburra laughed. He runs quickly.
Open the door. She made a cake.

A **compound verb** consists of two or more words.
He was waiting for me. I will make muffins.
She has been picking apples.

Circle the simple verbs in red and the compound verbs in blue.

Taylor is typing her assignment.

Snow fell heavily all night.

A bushfire is burning across the eastern ridge.

We will be leaving for Sydney early tomorrow morning. (See Processes p.71)

TRY THIS

Infinitives

An **infinitive** is a verb form.
It is usually introduced by the word 'to'.

For example: We went outside to play.
I want to buy a new car.

An infinitive needs another verb to make sense with a subject.

The children *had to* eat quickly and leave.
We *have to* wait until the sun goes down.

Infinitives can do the work of:

- **nouns** (tells what): I am learning to play the violin. To sleep is bliss.
- **adverbs** (tells why): I go to school to learn. I went to the river to swim.

As a general rule, we do not 'split' the infinitive (place a word between 'to' and the verb). For example, we say:
She decided to walk home slowly. NOT She decided to slowly walk home.
I want you to speak clearly. NOT I want you to clearly speak.

However, this is only a general rule. We just need to be sure that, if we do 'split' the infinitive, we do not change our meaning or make it unclear.

Verb categories

Verbs fall into different categories:
'doing' verbs 'saying' verbs 'thinking' verbs
'feeling' verbs 'being' verbs 'having' verbs

'Doing' verbs express action.
run, hop, skip, cook, read, sleep, buy

'Saying' verbs express ways of speaking.
shout, whisper, grumble

'Thinking' verbs express ways of thinking.
imagine, believe, wonder

'Feeling' verbs express ways of feeling.
like, sympathise, admire

TRY THIS

Find the verbs.

Leo shouted to his friends across the playground.
We enjoyed our picnic by the river.
The car screeched to a halt at the red light.
I wonder if Dad will burn the sausages again!

'Being' verbs include **am**, **is**, **are**, **was**, **were**.
They can be used on their own to link ideas together. These are **linking** verbs.

I am cold. He was friendly. This is my dog.

They can be used to 'help' other verbs.
(See Auxiliary verbs p.26)

I am waiting for the bus. She is reading a book.
They are playing hockey.
He was cooking sausages.

'Being' verbs also include **be**, **being** and **been**, but they can only be used with other verbs.

She will be home soon. You are being silly.
I have been to London.

'Having' verbs include **has**, **have** and **had**.
They can be used on their own.

He has five dollars. They have new uniforms.
We had a game of chess.

They can be used to 'help' other verbs.
(See Auxiliary verbs p.26)

He has done his homework. We have washed the dishes. Jo had lost her way.

Complete the sentences using 'being' or 'having' verbs.

She ___ sixteen years old today.

Sarah _____ a new pony.

The teacher _____ happy because we ______ early.

The players _____ special jerseys to wear for the final game.

Where ______ you last night?

Participles

Participles are forms of verbs. Verbs have two participles.
– a **present participle** and a **past participle**.
Participles need to work with 'helping' verbs to make sense. (See p.26)

Present participles end in the suffix **–ing**.
racing cooking falling swimming going washing driving

Present participles are used:

- as part of a compound verb to show continuous action:
  I was walking in the forest.
  Paul is riding to school. They are singing the National Anthem.
- to begin participial phrases (See p.46):
  Standing on tip-toe, I could see over Mr Brown's wall.

present participle:
falling leaves

Past participles are used:

- as part of a compound verb (See p.30):

They had walked to the waterfall. You could have waited for me. The sugar has dissolved quickly.

- to begin participial phrases (See p. 46):

Viewed from space, Earth looks like a blue and white ball.

Regular past participles end in the suffix **–ed**.
roasted boiled melted sailed watched printed folded

Some past participles are **irregular**.
They do not end in the suffix **–ed**.
ride – has ridden fall – has fallen
keep – has kept sing – has sung
draw – has drawn

Sometimes the base verb and the past participle are the same.
For example, we say 'I have cut the cake' not 'I have cutted the cake'.
We say 'She has put it away' not 'She has putted it away'.

MEET THE HELPERS!

am is are
was were
be being
been
do does did
has have had
shall will can
must may
might
could would
should

Auxiliary verbs

Auxiliary verbs are 'helping' verbs. They are used with other verbs or participles to make a complete verb.

For example: I *am* going to the movies tonight.
We *might* leave at three.
They *were* watching TV.
You *could have* waited for me!

Helping verbs give a more precise sense of time – current, past, ongoing, future – as well as showing obligation and possibility. (See Modality p.76)

Helping verbs show:

Present	We *are* eating dinner. I *am* listening to the news.
	She *is* counting her money.
Past	They *have* eaten a pizza.
	We *had* watched the weather report.
	He *was* climbing a tree.
Future	Dad *will* eat later. I *shall be* waiting for you.
Ability	I *can* play the piano. All of them *could* swim.
Possibility	Mia *may* go to Sydney next week. He *might* go too.
Obligation	You *must* stay inside. She *should be* saving her money.

The choice of helping verb can subtly change a message. Try some different helping verbs to change the meaning of these messages.

You ________________ wait for me.

Recycled water ________________ solve the problem of water shortages.

Scientists ________ discover life on other planets.

He ________________ not come.

Auxiliary verb, past tense: He was climbing a tree.

Negative verbs

A sentence can be made negative by placing **not** between the helping verb and the main verb.
For example: I could not catch him.
They will not win the game.
He does not like olives. We had not seen a hyena.

Contractions

In **negative** sentences, the helping verb and 'not' are often joined together, or contracted, to make one word.
This is called a **contraction**.

For example: did not = didn't
would not = wouldn't has not = hasn't

An apostrophe is used to mark the missing letter 'o'.

did not → didnot → didn't

Match the contractions with the words they replace.

doesn't	had not
won't	were not
hadn't	does not
weren't	will not

didn't	would not
wouldn't	was not
can't	can not
wasn't	did not

haven't	do not
aren't	have not
don't	could not
couldn't	are not

A pronoun subject and a helping verb often contract to make one word.

For example: it is = it's I will = I'll
we would = we'd

Contractions are most often used in speaking and informal writing.

An apostrophe is used to mark the missing letter or letters.

we will → we'll

she is → she's

he has → he's

COMMON CONTRACTIONS

I am	I'm	she is	she's	he is	he's
I have	I've	she has	she's	he has	he's
I had	I'd	she had	she'd	he had	he'd
I would	I'd	she would	she'd	he would	he'd
I will	I'll	she will	she'll	she will	she'll
you are	you're	we are	we're	they are	they're
you have	you've	we have	we've	they have	they've
you had	you'd	we had	we'd	they had	they'd
you would	you'd	we would	we'd	they would	they'd
you will	you'll	we will	we'll	they will	they'll
it is	it's	let us	let's	where is	where's
it has	it's	could have	could've	when is	when's
it would	it'd	should have	should've	what is	what's
it had	it'd	would have	would've	why is	why's
it will	it'll	here is	here's	what has	what's
that is	that's	there is	there's	who is	who's
that has	that's	there has	there's	who has	who's
that will	that'll	there had	there'd	who have	who've
that had	that'd	there would	there'd	who would	who'd
that would	that'd	there will	there'll	who will	who'll

Tense

Verbs tell us when things are happening.

in the present	in the past	in the future
A bird is flying.	A bird flew.	The bird will fly.

❖ How to write verbs in the present tense.

1. base verb
   - singular — He plays football.
   - plural — They play football.

2. present participle with a helper
   - singular — He is playing football.
   - plural — They are playing football.

❖ How to write verbs in the past tense.

1. base verb + ed
   - singular — He played football.
   - plural — They played football.

2. present participle with a helper
   - singular — He was playing football. He has been playing football.
   - plural — They were playing football. They have been playing football.

3. past participle with a helper
   - singular — He has played football.
   - plural — They have played football.

❖ How to write verbs in the future tense.

base verb with the helpers shall and will
- singular — We shall play football.
- plural — They will play football.

NOTE: may and might indicate a possible future.
eg He may play football. They might play football.

NOTE: Future tense can be shown in other ways.
eg I am going to play football. Tomorrow, I am playing football.
I am about to play football.

PRESENT TENSE VERBS

Tense	Number	1st person	2nd person	3rd person
Simple present	Singular	I eat fish	You eat fish.	He/she/it eats fish.
	Plural	We eat fish.	You eat fish.	They eat fish.
Present continuous	Singular	I am eating fish.	You are eating fish.	He/she/it is eating fish.
	Plural	We are eating fish.	You are eating fish.	They are eating fish.
Present perfect	Singular	I have eaten fish.	You have eaten fish.	He/she/it has eaten fish.
	Plural	We have eaten fish.	You have eaten fish.	They have eaten fish.
Perfect continuous	Singular	I have been eating fish.	You have been eating fish.	He/she/it has been eating fish.
	Plural	We have been eating fish.	You have been eating fish.	They have been eating fish.

PAST TENSE VERBS

Tense	Number	1st person	2nd person	3rd person
Simple past	Singular	I ate fish	You ate fish.	He/she/it ate fish.
	Plural	We ate fish.	You ate fish.	They ate fish.
Past continuous	Singular	I was eating fish.	You were eating fish.	He/she/it was eating fish.
	Plural	We were eating fish.	You were eating fish.	They were eating fish.
Past perfect	Singular	I had eaten fish.	You had eaten fish.	He/she/it had eaten fish.
	Plural	We had eaten fish.	You had eaten fish.	They had eaten fish.
Perfect continuous	Singular	I had been eating fish.	You had been eating fish.	He/she/it had been eating fish.
	Plural	We had been eating fish.	You had been eating fish.	They had been eating fish.

FUTURE TENSE VERBS

Tense	Number	1st person	2nd person	3rd person
Simple future	Singular	I will eat fish	You will eat fish.	He/she/it will eat fish.
	Plural	We will eat fish.	You will eat fish.	They will eat fish.
Future continuous	Singular	I will be eating fish.	You will be eating fish.	He/she/it will be eating fish.
	Plural	We will be eating fish.	You will be eating fish.	They will be eating fish.
Future perfect	Singular	I will have eaten fish.	You will have eaten fish.	He/she/it will have eaten fish.
	Plural	We will have eaten fish.	You will have eaten fish.	They will have eaten fish.
Perfect continuous	Singular	I will have been eating fish.	You will have been eating fish.	He/she/it will have been eating fish.
	Plural	We will have been eating fish.	You will have been eating fish.	They will have been eating fish.

We can add other verbs to clarify what we mean.

I **could** have been eating fish.
They **should** be eating fish.
He **might** have eaten fish.
We **can** eat fish.

Regular verbs

Regular verbs can have the suffixes **-s**, **-ing** and **-ed** added to them.

For example: visits, visiting, visited;
rains, raining, rained;
bakes, baking, baked

The suffix **-s** is added to most verbs in the 3rd person singular, so that subject and verb agree.
She skips. He hops. It chases.

The suffix **-es** is added to verbs ending in sh, ch, ss, zz and x.
washes watches misses buzzes fixes

The suffix **-ing** is added to a verb to form a present participle.

skipping hopping chasing camping

Remember → present participles must be used with helping verbs.

She is skipping. He was hopping.
They were chasing cats. We are camping.

The suffix **-ed** is added to the verb to form past tense verbs and past participles.

skipped hopped chased camped

Remember → past participles must be used with helping verbs.

She has skipped away. He had hopped away.
They had chased the cats. We have been camped for a week.

TRY THIS

Complete this table of regular verbs.

Verb	I am ...	Yesterday I ...	I have ...
cook	cooking	cooked	cooked
walk			
butter			
shout			
vote			
continue			

Irregular verbs

Irregular past tense verbs and past participles do not end in the suffix **-ed**.

For example: eat, ate, eaten; swim, swam, swum; do, did, done; see, saw, seen

Past tense verbs and past participles may be the same.
He left us behind. He had left us behind.
They stood up. They have stood up.

Past tense verbs and past participles may be different.

I drew a picture. She has drawn a picture.
I took a photo. I had taken a photo.

A small number of irregular verbs have the same form in the present and past tense and the past participle.

I cut bread. I cut the bread this morning.

Complete this table of irregular verbs.

Verb	I am ...	Yesterday I ...	I have ...
blow	blowing	blew	blown
begin			
lie*			
write			
ride			
hurt			
ring			
break			
shut			
slide			
know			
sing			
hit			

*Lie, as in 'lie down'.

NOTE: 'Lay' is commonly used wrongly in the present tense, for example 'Go and lay down.' This is incorrect. You cannot use 'lay down' in the present tense, only in the past tense.
So: 'Go and lie down.' 'I felt sick and had to lie down.'
OR 'I lay down on the grass.' 'I lay on my bed until I felt better.'

Finite and non-finite verbs

A **finite verb** is a verb that has a **subject** and gives a sentence meaning.
For example: Jake (subject) walks (verb) to school.

A **finite verb** can consist of one or more words.
Jake walks to school. Jake is walking to school.
Jake will walk to school. Jake was walking to school.
Jake has walked to school. Jake had walked to school.
Jake has been walking to school.

A **non-finite verb** is not a complete verb and does not make sense without a helping verb.

We can't say 'Jake walking to school' or 'Jake to walk to school'.
Participles and infinitives are non-finite verbs.

Subject agreement

The **verb** and its **subject** must always agree in number.
A singular subject needs a singular verb.
A plural subject requires a plural verb.

For example: Sam is eating lunch. They are eating lunch.
Jodi swims well. The children swim well.

It is often a 'helping' verb that shows agreement with the subject.

Singular 'helping' verbs		Plural 'helping' verbs	
Present tense	am, is, do, does, has, have	Present tense	are, have
Past tense	was, did, had	Past tense	were, did, had

For example:
Singular – I am leaving soon. Jesse is reading a magazine.
She does her homework every night. Jon has a rock collection. Bill was late for school.

Plural – The horses are galloping.
They were lost in the rainforest. We had fun.

Sometimes, the **subject** is not mentioned, but we understand what it is.

'Beat the butter and sugar until creamy.'
Here the subject is understood to be YOU – a cook reading a recipe.
Therefore the verb is singular.

Transitive and intransitive verbs

Transitive verbs pass the action from the subject to the object. (See p. 53)

For example: Karl (subject) built (verb) a model plane (object).
Jane (subject) was picking (verb) wildflowers (object).
I (subject) climbed (verb) the plum tree (object).

Intransitive verb: The birds flew away.

Intransitive verbs have a subject but no object.

For example: The children (subject) cheered (verb) loudly.
The birds (subject) flew (verb) away.
Snow (subject) is falling (verb) in the city.

Active and passive voice

The gardener planted roses. (active voice)

The roses were planted by the gardener. (passive voice)

Verbs can be **active** or **passive**.

A verb is **active** when the subject is doing the action.
For example: The gardener planted roses.

A verb is **passive** when the subject is NOT doing the action.
For example: The roses were planted by the gardener.

The most common way of writing a sentence is to have the subject of the sentence doing the action of the verb. This is called **active voice**.

Storms lashed the coast of Tasmania.
Thieves stole the money.
I baked bread.

A more impersonal way of writing is to have the subject receiving the action of the verb. This is called **passive voice**.

The Tasmanian coast was lashed by storms.
The money was stolen by thieves.

As we speak and write, we often change from active to passive voice.

The thieves stole the money and were arrested by the police.

In this example, the thieves steal the money, but the police do the arresting.

The focus of attention shifts as we use active or passive verbs.

Passive voice distances the subject from the action.

Compare:

'A car hit the dog'

and

'The dog was hit by a car'.

Newspaper reports are often deliberately written in an impersonal way to present unbiased accounts of events. (See Voice p.83)

Newspaper reports are often deliberately written in an impersonal way to present unbiased accounts of events.

Mood

Speakers and writers express **mood** through the sentence types they use. These are:

statements questions commands

Declarative mood is expressed through statements. (See pp.49, 75)

Statements can be either facts or opinions.

In writing, statements begin with capital letters and usually end in full stops.
Our team received the winner's trophy.
He was elected president of the USA.

Statements can be either facts or opinions.
Mushrooms have no flowers, seeds, leaves or roots. (fact)

The platypus is the world's oddest creature. (opinion)

Mushrooms have no flowers, seeds, leaves or roots. (fact)

Imperative mood is expressed through commands. The verbs usually appear first. The subject is often understood. (See pp.51, 75)

[You] Stir in the milk and flour.
[You] Fold the paper diagonally, corner to corner.
[You] Open the door please.

Imperative mood is used to give instructions or directions.

Interrogative mood is expressed through questions. (See pp.50,75)
In writing, sentences begin with a capital letter and end in a question mark.

Where have you been?
What is your favourite game?

When we ask a question beginning with a verb, the verb and its helper are usually separated by the subject.

Did you see the Grand Final?
Have they finished the game?
Can Blake skate? May I come too?

The platypus is the world's oddest creature. (opinion)

Tag questions are written as statements with a tag at the end.

You'll come with me, won't you?
The whale is the world's largest animal, isn't it?

Rhetorical questions are questions where an answer is not expected.

Me? sing on my own? You've got to be joking.
Can't come? That's disappointing.

Verb suffixes

Suffixes are syllables attached to the ends of words.
Some suffixes form verbs.

For example: illustrate strengthen televise notify sparkle

The most common verb suffixes are **-s**, **-ing**, **-d**, **-n**, **-ed** and **-en**. (See pp.25, 32)

We can change other word forms to verbs by adding particular suffixes.

sign (noun) signify (verb)

weak (adjective) weaken (verb)

Create verbs by adding suffixes.
***Watch your spelling.**

critic + ise		class + ify	
false + ify		wide + en	
flat + en		sterile + ise	

ADVERBS

Adverbs tell us how, when and where things happen

Adverbs are words that add meaning to the actions of people, places, events and objects.
They tell us how, when, where and for how long things happen.

Adverbs add meaning to:

- a verb – He runs quickly.
- an adjective – He is a very fast runner.
- another adverb – He runs too quickly for me.

NOTE: Adverbs add meaning to verbs, adjectives and other adverbs, NEVER to nouns.

(See Circumstances p.71)

NOTE: Some words ending in –ly are adjectives.

friendly man
early bird
curly hair
silly person

Adverbs of manner

Adverbs of manner tell us **how** something is being done.

For example: He nodded anxiously. He spoke slowly. I can run fast.

Adverbs of manner answer the question 'how' about the verb. The answer may follow the verb or may be elsewhere in the sentence.

The balloon rose effortlessly. He nodded his head slowly.

Many **adverbs of manner** end in the suffix **–ly**.

They are often built from adjectives.

quickly lazily fiercely silently busily angrily wistfully

TRY THIS

Change these adjectives to adverbs of manner by adding –ly.

silent	patient	loud	helpful	quiet	cold
clear	bad	quick	careless	noisy	recent

Adverbs of time

Adverbs of time tell us **when**, or for **how long**, something is being done.

For example: He arrived yesterday. She is arriving tomorrow.

Adverbs of time answer the question 'when' or 'for how long' about the verb. The answer may follow the verb or may be elsewhere in the sentence.

He seldom comes *to visit*. The race *occurs* annually. I haven't *seen* him lately.

Here is a list of common adverbs of time.

often	soon	later	seldom	occasionally
early	daily	annually	weekly	once
yesterday	tomorrow	sometimes	never	always
yet	rarely	immediately	regularly	then
after	afterwards	again	next	since

Adverbs of place

Adverbs of place tell us **where** something is, or is taking place.

For example: Here is the hat I lost. Put your school bag there by the door.

Adverbs of place answer the question 'where' about the verb. The answer may follow the verb or may be elsewhere in the sentence.

There it is! I can't find it anywhere.

TRY THIS

Find the adverbs of place in these sentences.

The plane flew high above the clouds. Finally it came down to land.
I will run away and hide somewhere. Then you can look for me.
I thought I left my hat here, but it is nowhere to be found.
Mum has gone out in the car and Dad is somewhere in the garden.
The birds flew off, but one was left behind.
In the marathon, Josh came first and I came tenth.

Interrogative adverbs

Adverbs that introduce questions are: How? When? Where? Why?

Adverbs can be used to introduce certain questions.
For example: When will you be leaving for Paris?

Adverbs that introduce questions are:
How? When? Where? Why?

These questions are very useful when researching a topic of study.

Where is the Eiffel Tower?
When was it built?
Why was it built?
How is it used today?

Modifiers and intensifiers

Adverbs add meaning to adjectives and other adverbs. These adverbs **modify** or **intensify** the meaning.

For example:
extremely fit very loudly (intensifiers)
fairly slow nearly there (modifiers)

Intensifier: immensely pleased

Modifiers weaken or soften a message, while **intensifiers** strengthen it. (See Modality p. 76)

Compare:

'The journey was quite long and rather tiring.'
and
'The journey was extremely long and very tiring.'

Compare:

'I am quite sure he is telling the truth.'
and
'I am absolutely sure he is telling the truth.'

Here are some examples of modifiers and intensifiers.

almost ripe	deeply troubled	really happy	fairly slowly
entirely wrong	somewhat concerned	unusually quiet	reasonably fast
quite old	wholly satisfied	immensely pleased	rather late

We use modifiers and intensifiers to make our messages clear. We use them particularly when we are trying to persuade others to a point of view – arguing or discussing issues, advertising products, making a complaint, or reviewing movies and books.

Adverbs of degree

Adverbs of degree show comparative differences in the time, place and manner in which things happen. For example: The balloon flew high. The helicopter flew higher. The jet flew highest of all.

There are three degrees:

- **positive** – says how, when, where or for how long something is happening. (Liam arrived early. He had not walked far.)
- **comparative** – shows a higher degree of difference, one to another. (Samuel arrived earlier than Liam. He had walked farther.)
- **superlative** – shows the highest degree of difference compared to all others. (Ned arrived earliest of them all. He had walked the farthest.)

Generally we add **–er** to show comparative degree and **–est** to show superlative degree.
long longer longest;
late later latest;
soon sooner soonest

Some adverbs of degree will look like adjectives, but remember adverbs do not add meaning to nouns, adjectives do.

We use **more** and **most** before adverbs ending in the suffix **–ly**.

anxiously more anxiously most anxiously
excitedly more excitedly most excitedly
happily more happily most happily

There are some **irregular** adverbs of degree.
well better best; much more most;
badly worse worst

Negative adverbs

Negative adverbs are used to make sentences negative.

For example: I do not agree.
They have not come yet.
He is not ready to go.

Negative adverb: Never come back here again!

In speech and informal writing, they are often written as contractions. (See p.28)

I don't agree. They haven't come yet.
He isn't ready to go.

Never can also be used to make a sentence negative.

She is never on time.
Never come back here again!

Affirmative adverbs

Affirmative adverbs give messages a positive feel.

For example: yes, certainly, surely, undoubtedly

Antonyms

Adverbs can show opposing information about verbs. These adverbs are called **antonyms**.

For example: Was she speaking loudly or softly?

Write the antonyms for these adverbs.

sadly		inside	
now		smoothly	
tightly		always	
badly		weakly	
high		above	
quietly		sooner	

PHRASES

Phrases add meaning and detail to sentences

A phrase is a group of words that only makes sense within a sentence, never on its own.
We speak in phrases, giving speech its sense of rhythm.

For example: under a chair, over the hill, in the forest, after school

A phrase has NO verb and NO subject, but it DOES give important detail to what we say and write. Look at all the information we are given through the phrases in this sentence:

Jack and Jill went up the hill and down the lane, through the park and over the fence, across the paddock, among the cows, past the gate … and climbed up the apple tree. (See p.73)

Prepositions

A **phrase** is often introduced by a **preposition**. Prepositions position people or objects in space and time.
For example: under a chair, over the hill, in the forest, after school

TRY THIS

Here is a list of prepositions. Can you think of some phrases introduced by these prepositions?

aboard	at	down	of	to
about	before	during	off	towards
above	behind	except	on	under
across	below	for	over	until
after	beneath	from	past	up
against	beside	in	since	upon
along	between	into	through	with
among	by	near	throughout	without
around			till	

Participial phrases

A **phrase** is often introduced by a **participle**.
(See p.25)

For example:
Standing on tip-toes, I could just see over the wall.
Viewed from space, Earth looks like a blue and white ball.

Present participles are built from verbs and end in **-ing**.
walking cooking staring looking speeding

Past participles are built from verbs and generally end in **-ed**.
stored potted saved branded painted

Underline the participial phrases in these sentences.

Standing waist-deep in water, Sam signalled for help.

Crowded with people, the bus set off down the dusty road.

The students, dressed in school uniform, arrived at the museum.

Waiting for me was my father, holding a bunch of flowers.

I just love pancakes, buttered thickly.

Adjectival phrases

Adjectival phrases do the same work as **adjectives**.

For example: the girl with blue eyes
a box of chocolates the bird in the cage

Adjectival phrase: the girl with blue eyes

Adjectival phrases can begin with:

- Prepositions – a note from her mother; the orchids in the greenhouse
- Infinitives – a message to abort the landing; a scarf to wear in winter

It is important to place the adjectival phrase near to the noun it describes.

The students went to see the elephants in broad-brimmed hats. ✗
The students, in broad-brimmed hats, went to see the elephants. ✓
In broad-brimmed hats, the students went to see the elephants. ✓

(See p.73)

Circle the nouns which the adjectival phrases describe.

Please wash the cups on the sink.

The bell above the door is made of brass.

Will you help me carry this box of books?

He chose the chocolate in the gold wrapper.

The man with the sunburnt face is a fisherman.

Adverbial phrases

Adverbial phrases do the same work as **adverbs**.

For example: He ran past the gate.
The sun sets in the west.
After school, we play cricket.
I am waiting for my friends.

Like adverbs, adverbial phrases add information about HOW, WHEN, WHERE, WHY or FOR HOW LONG things happen. (See p.73)

On Christmas morning, I woke in great excitement. (how)

Within minutes, the ship sank to the bottom of the sea. (how long)

They dived beneath the waves in search of the wrecked ship. (where)

Wait for me! (why)

On Saturday afternoon, we are going to watch the Grand Final. (when)

Add adverbial phrases to give more information about the verb.

The train will leave the station ______________________. (when)

Lean your bike ______________________. (where)

The soldier received a medal ______________________. (why)

He spoke ______________________. (how)

The storm continued ______________________. (how long)

Noun phrases

Noun phrases do the same work as **nouns**.

For example: Saving water is important.
I like climbing trees.

Noun phrases usually answer the question WHAT.
(See p.73)

They can be the **subject** of a sentence.

Walking every day is good exercise.

They can be the **object** of a sentence.

Tom Roberts enjoyed painting landscapes.

Underline the noun phrases in these sentences.

Riding skateboards is not allowed in the shopping mall.

Smithy's dream was to fly solo across the Tasman Sea.

Climbing Mt Everest was Sir Edmund Hilary's greatest achievement.

We must learn to care for each other.

Playing a musical instrument requires a lot of practice.

SENTENCES

A sentence contains a complete idea and makes sense

A sentence is a meaningful unit of language, complete in itself. It has at least one verb and makes sense.

For example: Humpty Dumpty sat on a wall.
Have you heard the news? Come with me.
Everyone was there when I arrived.

Sentences are the building blocks of our spoken and written language and it is through them that we understand each other and the world.
It is through sentences that we interact with each other, statement by statement and question by answer.

In spoken language we use rising and falling intonation through the phrases and mark our sentences with pauses. Gestures and facial expressions fill in the gaps. Answers to questions are often given in sentence fragments, but can still be understood.

In written language, we begin our sentences with capital letters and mark the end with full stops, question marks or exclamation marks.

We use speech marks to show dialogue and bullet points to introduce lists.

We use
"speech marks"
to show dialogue
and
• bullet points
to introduce
lists.

Statements

Many sentences are **statements**.
Statements declare facts or ideas.
For example: The price of oil has risen sharply.

A written statement begins with a capital letter and ends with a full stop. Statements may be facts, which can be proven, or the opinions of the speaker or writer. (See pp. 37, 38, 75)
He is entering university this year. (fact)
Uniforms should be worn in all schools. (opinion)

Questions

Many sentences ask **questions** and usually expect answers.

For example: Would you like a game of tennis? What is a glacier?

A written **question** begins with a capital letter and ends with a question mark. (See pp. 38, 75) Questions can begin with an interrogative adjective, adverb or pronoun.

Where did you find my keys? Whose are these? Which shirt do you like?

Rhetorical questions ask questions but don't expect an answer.

Tag questions are statements with a tag on the end.

You will buy a ticket, won't you? They went swimming, didn't they?

Rhetorical questions ask questions but don't expect an answer.

Me? Sing on my own? You've got to be joking. Can't come? That's disappointing.

Exclamations

Many sentences express sudden surprise, joy or fright. These are **exclamations**.

For example: Stop! Help! I don't believe it! Hurray!

A written **exclamation** begins with a capital letter and ends with an exclamation mark. Exclamation marks also follow **interjections** – remarks made to interrupt a dialogue.

Oh! Goodness me! Whoops!

If the exclamation is also a question, the exclamation mark is placed after the question mark.

You want me to do what?!
You're leaving school?!

Commands

Many sentences give **commands** and expect action.

For example: Close the door please.
Add one cup of flour.
Return all your books to the library.

Recipes and instructions are mostly written as a series of commands.

Commands request or demand an action from the listener or reader.

In written language, commands begin with a capital letter and end with a full stop or exclamation mark.

Commands usually begin with a verb in the present tense. The subject is usually understood and therefore not mentioned.

For example: [You] Get ready for school.
Bake in a hot oven for ten minutes.
Cut out all the pictures on the page.
Don't forget to bring a raincoat.
Switch on the light, please.
Get out! And don't come back! (See pp. 38, 75)

Recipes and instructions are mostly written as a series of commands.

Say whether the sentences are statements, questions, exclamations or commands.

Sign your name at the bottom of the page. ________________

Cocoa trees grow only near the equator. ________________

What time is dinner? ________________

Bend the wire to make a hook. ________________

What?! You left your hat on the bus! ________________

Subject and predicate

A sentence has two parts:
a **subject** – who or what the sentence is about; and
a **predicate** – what is said about the subject.
The predicate always includes the verb.

For example: The small plane (subject) flew low over the city (predicate).

To find the subject, ask 'who' or 'what' before the verb.

A **subject** consists of a noun, noun group or pronoun. (See p.70)
Bees (subject) are kept in a hive.
Yellow honey bees (subject) are kept in a hive.
They (subject) are kept in a hive.

The subject is generally placed before the verb.

To find the subject, ask 'who' or 'what' before the verb.

The **subject** is not always placed at the beginning of a sentence.
An exploding volcano (subject) often sends out a cloud of poisonous gases.
Faster and faster, the skier (subject) sped down the mountain slope.

Sometimes the subject is not stated, but we understand what it is.
Wait for me. (subject, 'you')
Fold the paper in half. (subject, 'you')

What is the subject of each sentence?

The hot air balloon floated high in the sky.

Every year, I receive a birthday card from my English cousin.

Golden autumn leaves fall gently to the ground.

Faster and faster, the go-kart rolled down the hill.

Pour the mixture into a tray.

Object

Sometimes a verb has both a 'doer' (the **subject**) and a 'receiver' (the **object**).
The action is passed from the subject to the object through the verb.

For example: The crow (subject) snatched the mouse (object).

The **object** lies within the predicate and consists of a noun, noun group or pronoun. (See p.70)

A sentence always has a subject, but may not have an **object**.
The crowd (subject) cheered loudly.
The boys (subject) raced to the river.

A subject may have a **direct object**.
To find the direct object, ask 'who' or 'what' after the verb.
Dad (subject) pitched the tent (direct object) under the gum tree.
Kookaburras (subject) eat fish, frogs and insects (direct object).

A verb may have an **indirect object**.
This is the person or thing affected by the action of the verb.
The librarian (subject) gave the girl (indirect object) a book (direct object).
In this sentence it is the book that the librarian gives, not the girl.
Therefore, book is the direct object.

To find the direct object, ask 'who' or 'what' after the verb.

TRY THIS

Does every sentence have an object? Are the objects direct or indirect objects?

The clowns tumbled round the circus ring.

We bought tickets to the Grand Final.

Mum packed a picnic lunch.

Bobby knocked loudly on the door.

Give this box to Julie.

Simple sentences

A **simple sentence** consists of one **principal** clause. It has a verb and a subject. (See pp.63, 74)

Wild birds come to feed in my back garden.
We have singing practice before school.

It is common in simple sentences to place the subject before the verb. The verb can be simple or compound.
The horse (subject) galloped (simple verb) round the race track.
Scientists (subject) have discovered (compound verb) a new planet.

The verb can also be placed before its subject.
Standing at the door was (verb) my best friend (subject).

Compound sentences

A **compound sentence** must have two (or more) principal clauses. A **conjunction** joins them together. (See pp. 64, 74)

Pia lives in Windsor Street and she drives a sporty, red car.
Amy likes chicken, but I prefer fish.

Conjunctions are sometimes called joining words. They include the words and, but, or, so and yet.

Conjunctions are sometimes called joining words. They include the words **and**, **but**, **or**, **so** and **yet**.
Jake drove the car and Mary read the map.
I'd like to go to the football game, but I don't have a ticket.
Jane is coming over, so we can play chess.
Would you like to read, or do you want to play Monopoly?
It was late at night, yet the weather remained warm and humid.

TRY THIS

Join these simple sentences to make compound sentences.
Jess has an appointment at two o'clock. She must leave early.
I would like to buy this jacket. It is too expensive.
Would you like orange juice? Would you prefer lemonade?

Complex sentences

A **complex sentence** is made up of a **principal** clause and one or more **subordinate** clauses. (See p. 63)

Check the depth of the pool (principal) before you dive in (subordinate).

A subordinate clause can begin with a **conjunction**. (See pp. 64, 67, 74)

When the river flooded, many properties were damaged.
Beetles keep their wings folded unless they are flying.

A subordinate clause can begin with a **relative pronoun**.

The relative pronouns are **who** and **whom** (used when talking about people) and **which** and **that** (used when talking about animals and things).
Mozart was a composer who wrote many wonderful pieces of music.
Is this the chess piece that you lost?
I made a mud cake, which everyone enjoyed.

Subordinate clauses that do the work of **adverbs** can be placed:

- at the beginning of a sentence followed by a comma:
  When he finished reading his book, he returned it to the library.
- in the middle of a sentence (an embedded clause) enclosed by commas:
  The first books, as far as anyone knows, were made in Egypt.
- at the end of a sentence (See pp. 64, 65)
  I will make the beds while you cook breakfast.

Subordinate clauses that do the work of **adjectives** always follow the nouns they describe. (See p.65)
Jack Donahue was a bushranger who was nicknamed 'The Wild Colonial Boy'.
This is my new watch, which was a gift from my aunt.

Add subordinate clauses to make complex sentences.

We had to go inside when …

I will go if …

We go to our music lesson then …

An acrobat is a person who …

This is a bird that …

Word order

Sentences can begin with verbs, adjectives, adverbs, adverbial phrases, adverbial clauses, noun phrases and noun clauses.

The order of words, phrases and clauses in sentences can be varied to add colour and interest to what we say and write.

In English, the **subject** is generally placed before the verb.

The frightened rabbit (subject) scurried (verb) down into its burrow.

However, the verb can precede its subject.

Down into its burrow, scurried (verb) the frightened rabbit (subject).

Sentences can begin with **verbs**. Here the subject is understood.

Write your name on your book. (Subject 'you' understood)

Sentences can begin with **adjectives**.

Ripe and juicy, the plums hung invitingly from the branches.

Sentences can begin with **adverbs**. Place a comma after the adverb.

Suddenly, the seagulls swarmed round the fishing boat.

Ripe and juicy, the plums hung invitingly from the branches.

Sentences can begin with **adverbial phrases**. This can make a sentence more exciting. Place a comma after the phrase.

Faster and faster, the cyclist sped round the final bend.

Sentences can begin with **adverbial clauses**. Place a comma after the clause.

When you have finished your homework, you may go out to play.

Sentences can begin with **noun phrases**.

Collecting stamps is my favourite hobby.

Sentences can begin with **noun clauses**.

Who was leading the bike race was impossible to tell. (See p. 78)

Direct speech

Sentences can directly record the speech of one person to another. This is called **direct speech** or **dialogue**.

"I went to Darwin last holidays," said Finn.
"Was it hot there?" asked Rhys.

In writing, direct speech is shown by placing **speech marks** around the spoken words.
Speech marks may be called **inverted commas**.
"Will you sponsor me in my Walk against Want?" asked Todd.
"Yes," said Mrs Jiggs, "I'll give you $2 per kilometre."

Speech marks may be called inverted commas.

Things to remember:

1 The first spoken word has a capital letter.
Stan muttered, "No-one ever listens to me."
"Wait here for the storm to pass," advised the teacher.

2 Spoken words are separated from unspoken words by a comma, a question or exclamation mark.
"What can you tell me about the moon?" asked Mr Tibbs.
"It's a satellite of the Earth," Bill answered immediately.
"Yeah," Brad mocked, "and it's made of cheese!"

3 Each new speaker is given a new line.
"Have you read the latest *Gordon Black* novel?" asked Todd.
"No," sighed Sue.
"I haven't been able to buy a copy anywhere!" lamented Ned.

Indirect speech

Sentences can indirectly record what has been said.

Finn said that he had gone to Darwin last holidays.
Rhys asked him if it had been hot there.

Indirect speech is usually reported by an onlooker or third person, not the speaker. It is therefore written as a noun clause. (See pp. 66, 73)

"Oh! I hate mice!" Ella said to Kim.
(direct speech – Ella is speaking)
Ella told Kim that she hated mice. (indirect speech – reported by another person)

Indirect speech places the report into the past tense, making it narrative rather than drama. Indirect speech gives you the gist of what is said, rather than the actual words. Therefore speech marks are not needed.

We usually use indirect speech when reporting what other people say. Gossip is often passed on in indirect speech.

Change these statements from direct to indirect speech.
Carol said, "I've lost my earrings."
"The robber escaped with a diamond necklace," Mr Jack reported.
"Have you read *The Water Horse*?" Anthony asked Patrick.
The teacher said to the class, "Open your books at page six."

Person

Speakers and writers create language from three different points of view:
first person   second person   third person

First person:
I eat my greens.

First person point of view is when a writer, speaker or character is doing the 'talking'.
First person pronouns are used. (See p.18)
I eat my greens. We are going for a holiday with our cousins.

Second person point of view is used when someone is spoken to.
Second person pronouns are used. (See p. 18)
If you look, you will see your hat.

Third person point of view is used when writers and speakers talk about other people and things.
Third person pronouns are used. (See p.18)
They left him behind with their teacher.

Paragraphs

Paragraphs consist of any number of sentences, grouped around a single main idea.

Paragraphs are the large building blocks of written language, a bundling together of ideas. Consisting of a few sentences (usually no more than ten), each paragraph develops a particular point.

In narrative writing, the paragraphs help build the storyline. A paragraph can signal a change in events, settings or time. It can show the introduction of new characters or an exchange between known characters.

A paragraph can signal a change in events, settings or time.

In factual writing, each paragraph holds a unit of information. The paragraph begins with an idea or topic and the following sentences add the details. **The first sentence is often referred to as the topic sentence.**

For example:

Kookaburras

The kookaburra is a native Australian bird. Its name comes from the Aboriginal word meaning 'laughing bird'. It is the largest bird in the kingfisher family.

The kookaburra is a medium-sized bird, brown and white in colour with pale blue on the wing. It has a long beak and strong head and neck muscles. It has four claws on each foot, three in the front and one at the back.

Kookaburras eat caterpillars, fish, frogs, insects and small mammals, snakes, worms and other small birds. They are able to break open ants' nests with their strong beaks.

The kookaburra has a distinctive bird call, which sounds like laughter. When one kookaburra begins laughing, all the others join in, filling the air with kookaburra roundelays.

Connectives

Connectives are words and phrases that link ideas within sentences and across paragraphs.

Connectives set up relationships between the ideas on either side of them. These relationships are important in understanding what is being said, and for creating texts that are cohesive.
(See p.80)

Sequence		
first (second, third...)	finally	then
when	next	now
at this point	lastly	until then
meanwhile	previously	in the end
straightaway	at once	afterwards
on another occasion	next time	before that
at this moment	later	soon
Cause and effect		
consequently	therefore	then
as a consequence of	though	although
accordingly	nevertheless	because
as a result of	despite this	so as
under the circumstances	however	yet
an upshot of	even though	moreover
an outcome of	otherwise	in that case
all the same	an effect of	still
stemmed from	caused by	hence
Comparison and contrast		
however	nevertheless	instead
in spite of this	rather	also
on the other hand	differs from	elsewhere
alternatively	in that respect	on the contrary
whereas	in other respects	despite
notwithstanding	albeit	aside from

Addition		
furthermore	as well	besides
also	not only but …	while
along with	in addition	neither nor …
additionally	and	moreover
likewise		

Examples and results		
for example	for instance	as a result
such as	as exemplified by	therefore
these include	for one thing	thus
accordingly	consequently	through
hence	as a guide	by way of illustration

Punctuation

Punctuation marks are 'road signs' for readers. Punctuation marks show readers where statements and questions begin and end; and where they need to pause to make sense of the phrases and clauses.

Capital letters are used for:

- the first word in a sentence
  Come to the circus with me.
- proper names
  Cinderella danced with Prince Charming.
- the first spoken word in dialogue
  He said, "Let's play cricket."
- to emphasise important words
  You did WHAT?

Full stops end statements and commands.
That is a fine straw hat. Put it on, please.

Question marks end questions.
How long will you be away?

Exclamation marks end exclamations.
What! Late again! You did what?!

Capital letters are used for: the first word in a sentence, proper names, the first spoken word in dialogue and to emphasise important words.

Commas are used to separate:

- words in a list
  I like apples, pears, plums and grapes.
- a beginning phrase
  Later that day, we went for a swim.
- a beginning clause
  When I broke my leg, I used crutches.
- an embedded phrase
  Jean, waving her umbrella, hurried away.
- an embedded clause
  My dog, which is old now, still does tricks.
- spoken and unspoken words
  "A dingo is a wild dog," said Bradley.

Speech marks are used around spoken words.
"Dinner is on the table," called Brenda.
Remember: NEW speaker NEW line.
"Thanks. I'm coming," said Brenda;
"Me too!" shouted Jack.

Apostrophes are used:

- with nouns to show possession.
  Joe's toys dog's collar teachers' staffroom.
- to contract pronoun subjects and helping verbs.
  I've packed lunch. You're invited. It's fun.
- to contract helping verbs and negatives
  He can't swim. I couldn't sing. Don't shout.

A **semicolon** is used:

- to mark a break in a sentence. It is stronger than a comma and links ideas.
  My first attempt was a disaster; next time it will be better.

A **colon** is used:

- after a character's name in a script.
  THE GIANT: You thief! Come back!
  JACK: Come on big guy! Catch me if you can!
- to introduce a list of items.
  (A bullet point often precedes each item.)

  You will need to bring:
  - a raincoat
  - stout walking shoes
  - extra food

CLAUSES

A clause is a group of words with a subject and something to say about the subject.

For example: Dad and I went fishing.
The athlete won a gold medal.

A clause has a subject and says something about it

There are two types of **clauses**:

A **principal**, or **main**, clause consists of one complete idea.

Jillian made a model plane.

There on the doorstep was Rusty, waiting patiently.

A **simple sentence** consists of just one principal clause. (See pp. 54, 74)

A **subordinate**, or **dependent**, clause says more about the main idea in the principal clause. It is linked to the principal clause by a conjunction, or relative pronoun.

(See p. 67)

Alexander Bell was the person (principal) who invented the telephone (subordinate).

Before I go to bed, (subordinate) I clean my teeth (principal).

Notice how subordinate clauses, highlighted in the sentences above, are incomplete and do not make sense on their own.

A **complex sentence** consists of a principal clause and one or more subordinate clauses.

(See pp. 54, 74)

Before I go to bed,
(subordinate clause)
I clean my teeth.
(principal clause)

Conjunctions

A subordinate clause is joined to a principal clause by a **subordinating conjunction**. (See p. 68)

For example: My dog follows me (principal) wherever I go (subordinate).
We won't go (principal) if you are too tired (subordinate).

These are the conjunctions we most often use to join subordinate clauses.

after	as	although	and	before
because	but	if	once	then
though	therefore	until	unless	where
wherever	when	whenever	while	whilst

Relative pronouns

Relative pronouns are words we use to link the subordinate clause and the principal clause.

These are the boys (principal) who built the raft. (subordinate)
It was a song (principal) that everyone knew. (subordinate)

Relative pronoun: This is the picture that I have been painting.

There are five relative pronouns:

- **who** and **whom** used when talking about people; and the possessive **whose**.

A pilot is a person who flies planes.
You gave the book to whom?
The man, whose book I borrowed, has left town.

- **which** and **that** used when talking about things; and the possessive **whose**.

Here is your hat, which you left in the playground.
This is the picture that I have been painting.
The book, whose pages are torn, is in the bin.

Adverbial clauses

Many subordinate clauses do the work of adverbs. They tell us more about the verb.

He went to bed because he was tired.
Although she played well, she was not picked for the team.

Like adverbs, adverbial clauses tell us how, when, where, why or for how long things happen. (See p. 75)

They are linked to the principal clause by conjunctions. (See pp. 64, 67, 68)

What do the adverbial clauses tell us? How? When? Where? Why? How long?

I will make the toast while Dad cooks the eggs.
Charlotte knows a great spot where we can have a picnic.
After I get dressed for school, I will make my lunch.
I won't go unless you come with me.
We cheered until the players left the field.

Adverbial clauses can be placed at the beginning of a sentence, in the middle, or at the end.
(See pp. 55, 75)

When he finished reading his book, he returned it to the library.
Thomas, although he tried his best, failed to make the team.
I will make the beds while you cook breakfast.

Adjectival clauses

Many subordinate clauses do the work of adjectives. They tell us more about people and things.
For example: Bell is the man who invented the telephone.
It was a meteor that flashed across the sky.

Adjectival clauses always follow the nouns they describe. (See pp.55, 75)
They are linked to the principal clause by the relative pronouns:who, whom, which, that. (See p.64)

Underline the noun or pronoun that the adjectival clause describes.

The planet, which has just been discovered, may contain life.
A geologist is a person who studies rocks.
It is an invention that could change the way we shop.
Mr Brodie picked all the peaches that were ripe.
He discovered a fossil, which the museum could not identify.

Noun clauses

Many subordinate clauses do the work of nouns. Noun clauses usually tell WHAT someone is thinking, saying or feeling.

For example: He asked me what the time was.
People once believed that the world was flat.

Notice how the verb changes to past tense in indirect speech.

We often use noun clauses in **indirect speech**.
(See pp. 57, 58, 75)
Emma said, "I am feeling very nervous." (direct speech)
Emma said that she was feeling very nervous. (indirect speech)

After I won the trophy, Dad said, "I'm proud of you." (direct speech)
After I won the trophy, Dad said (that) he was proud of me. (indirect speech).
'That' is often omitted.
Notice how the verb changes to past tense in indirect speech.

Noun clauses can be placed anywhere in a sentence.
What I like is the way you speak so politely.
I had a feeling that everyone's eyes were on me.

Find the noun clauses in these sentences.

He pretended that he was asleep.

You can tell that I've never done this before!

That you lost your tennis match is hard to believe.

I told the police I didn't know anyone by that name.

Where I put my glasses is still a mystery.

CONJUNCTIONS

Conjunctions are joining words. They join ideas together in a meaningful way.

A conjunction joins ideas together in a meaningful way

Co-ordinating conjunctions join words that are the same.

- **Nouns** – Jack and Jill tea or coffee money for lunch
- **Adjectives** – tired but happy ripe and juicy yellow or orange
- **Adverbs** – here and there fast or slow quickly but carefully
- **Pronouns** – she and I us or them no-one but me

Co-ordinating conjunctions join phrases.

Sue went *up the steps* and *into the house.*

They battled *across the raging river* and *up the steep, slippery bank.*

Co-ordinating conjunctions join simple sentences to make compound sentences.

Jack is leaving now but he'll be back later.

Sarah is going to Melbourne and I'm going with her.

It is getting dark, so I'll walk home with you.
(See p.54)

Co-ordinating conjunctions include:
and, but, for, yet, so, or, nor

Co-ordinating conjunction: tired but happy

Correlative conjunctions are used in pairs.

I don't know whether to go to the skate park or to the movies.

Both Angela and Carol left early.

Neither Ayeng nor Agok was born in Australia.
(See p. 54)

Correlative conjunctions include: **whether...or, both...and, as...as, either...or, neither...nor, not...but, not only...but also**

Subordinating conjunction: When the lights went out, we lit a candle.

Subordinating conjunctions are used to link a subordinate clause to a principal clause.

She was late because she lost her way.

I will wait until my friends arrive.

When the lights went out, we lit a candle.

I'll look after the animals while you're away.

We'll have lunch, then we'll go for a walk.
(See p. 55)

Subordinating conjunctions include: **after, as, although, before, once, because, then, though, therefore, until, unless, where, wherever, when, whenever, while**

Introduction to Functional Grammar

Language is an integral part of our culture and lifestyle. We use it to express ourselves, to meet our needs, to give and receive information, and generally, to understand the world we live in. Most communication is driven by purpose, and language provides us with a vast array of 'tools' to help us achieve those purposes. We are constantly making language choices to express ourselves appropriately and effectively.

Language has three main functions:

- an **experiential function** – ways of representing our experiences
- an **interpersonal function** – ways of interacting with others
- a **textual function** – ways of constructing messages

To make meaning using our language, we make choices about:

- **field** – what we want to talk about
- **tenor** – who our audience is
- **mode** – how we will exchange the message.

Functional grammar describes how these choices are represented. It focuses on the different contributions made by clause, phrase, group and word structures.

FIELD	TENOR	MODE
the WHAT experiential function	the WHO interpersonal function	the HOW textual function
participants processes circumstances attributes phrases/groups clauses	mood modality attitude	theme and rheme cohesion voice nominalisation

Experiential function

Participants

Participants are the people, animals or objects that are involved in the events in text.
They are realised through **pronouns** and **noun groups**.

the noisy, old, alarm clock

A noun group is a group of words built around a noun. The noun is the head word and any other words build up a picture of that noun. (See p. 9)

the clock	six tomatoes
the alarm clock	six, red tomatoes
the noisy, old, alarm clock	six, firm, red tomatoes

Noun groups are used to name the **participants** in events. We are constantly composing text around them.

Participants are usually **subjects** or **objects**. (See pp. 52, 53)
The tiny, black spider (subject) is spinning (process) a tiny, silver web (object).
The members of the football team (subject) are flying (process) to Adelaide.
We (subject) boarded (process) the old, red school bus (object).
I (subject) tossed (process) some bread (object) to the ducks in the pond.

TRY THIS

Underline the participants in these passages.

The three, inexperienced schoolboys became lost in the rainforest. Many local people helped to search for them. They found the cold, hungry and frightened boys sixteen hours later.

The day of the Grand Final arrived. We entered the dressing rooms feeling both nervous and excited. After our warm-up and some final words from the captain, we jogged out onto the field. The crowd cheered and waved flags. Some of our supporters held banners and slogans. Some had painted their faces in our team's colours! We faced our opponents, full of excitement and confidence.

Processes

Processes tell us what the participants 'are' or are 'doing' in text. They are realised through **verbs** and **verb groups**.

Processes include:

- **action** processes
  run skate climb taste grow sparkle
- **saying** processes
  complain speak call whisper shout
- **thinking or feeling** processes
  imagine wonder believe like weep
- **being** processes
  am is are was were be being been
- **having** processes
  has have had

Processes are written as **simple verbs** or **verb groups**. (See p.23)
Betty painted her bedroom.
John was waiting for the bus to come.
Eddie has been practising the piano for an hour.
Will you come to the skate park with me?

Underline the processes. State what type of processes they are.

To earn some pocket money, David washes cars and cleans windows.
We had been wondering where to go for our holidays.
What are you mumbling about?
Philip will be sixteen next birthday.
A shark has razor-sharp teeth.

Circumstances

Circumstances tell us how, when, where, why or for how long things happen. They elaborate on the circumstances surrounding events. They are realised through **adverbs** and **adverbial phrases**.

Circumstances add information about, or **modify**, the processes through **adverbs** telling:

- **how** — The wind blew hard. A snail moves slowly.
- **how long** — Water dripped constantly from the tap.
- **when** — I'm going home soon. Come immediately.
- **where** — Put it there, please. I can't see it anywhere.

Circumstances add information about, or **modify**, processes through **adverbial phrases** telling:

- **how** — He spoke in a soft voice.
- **how long** — Boil the water for five minutes.
- **when** — During the night, a storm brought strong winds and hail.
- **where** — Let's go swimming in the river.
- **why** — I'm going to the shop for some milk.

Complete each sentence by adding a circumstance.

The long, cattle truck made its way ____________________. (where)

________________ the scouts returned from their hike. (when)

He spoke too ____________________. (how)

Stir the vegetables in the pan ________________________. (how long)

Let's go to McDonald's ____________________________. (why)

(See pp.40, 41, 47)

Attributes

Attributes add meaning to nouns. They elaborate on the qualities of the participants. They are realised through **adjectives** and **adjectival phrases**.

Adjectives give more information about nouns.

a sunny day   red roses   a few, green tomatoes

They are often an integral part of a noun group.

Strong, fierce tigers roam through the *dense* jungle.
You will need a *long* paintbrush and *some thick, red* paint.

Add two attributes (adjectives) to each sentence.

I would like a cup of ________, __________ coffee.

On __________, __________ days, I like to play mini golf.

The ________, __________ workers stopped for lunch.

I have never seen such __________, __________ country.

This is my __________, _________ dog.

Adjectival phrases give more information about nouns.

The *man* draped in the flowing, red cape is a magician.
The *dancer*, in a short, pink dress, twirled across the stage.

Underline the participants that the attributes (adjectival phrases) say more about.

The baby fox, feeling lost and lonely, huddled among the rocks.

The clown in baggy green trousers tumbled across the circus ring.

The letter from Aunty Emma was full of good news.

I bought a box of chocolates for my dad.

The man with the bald head stepped from the bus. (See p.46)

Phrases

A **phrase** is a group of words used within a larger unit of language. We use phrases to say more about the participants, processes and circumstances.

Phrases provide us with the 'tools' we need to:

- construct participants — **noun phrase** (See p. 48)
  a group of words built around the head word, which is a noun.
  For example: several, ripe, red tomatoes
- place events in time — **verb phrase** (See pp. 23, 26, 27)
  a group of words built around the head word, which is a verb.
  For example: could have been won
- modify events — **adverb phrase** (See p. 47)
  a group of words built around the head word, which is an adverb.
  For example: very slowly
- qualify processes — **preposition phrase** (See p. 45)
  a group of words made up of a preposition and a noun group
  For example: inside the dark, musty cave
- qualify participants — **adjectival phrase** (See p. 46)
  a group of words built around the head word, which is an adjective.
  For example: really beautiful

Clauses

A **clause** is a unit of meaning grouped around a process. Essentially, we speak and write by forming clauses and joining them in various ways.

For example:

It is Tim's birthday and he is having a party.
We had to wait until the plane arrived.

A **clause** can make sense on its own.

It was a large, carved wooden box with a curved lid and shiny brass latches.

More often, clauses combine to form **clause complexes**. These are usually called by the traditional term, **sentences**. (See p. 49)

There are three types of sentence or clause complexes.

1 Simple sentences comprise one clause that makes sense on its own. (See p. 54)

The two children moved cautiously towards the heavy, wooden door.

2 Compound sentences must include two or main clauses joined by a conjunction. Each clause could stand on its own. One of the clauses may expand on the other: (See pp. 54, 67)

Long ribbons of mist snaked through the trees and swirled round the forlorn old house.

or it may contain direct speech:

Chris tugged at her arm and whispered, "What is it? What can you see?"

3 Complex sentences comprise a main or principal clause and one or more dependent or subordinate clauses. A main clause makes sense by itself, but a dependent clause relies on the main clause to give it meaning. (See pp. 55, 63)

They looked back down the path, (main clause) which led to the old iron gate. (dependent clause)

Dependent clauses may function as:

- **adverb clauses**, which indicate how, when, where, why or for how long about the process in another clause.
  The children ***felt*** uneasy as the mist swirled silently around them.
- **adjective clauses**, which expand on the participant in another clause.
  The ***tree***, which had been struck by lightning, lay on the ground.
- **noun clauses**, which report on the words or thoughts of a human participant in another clause. This is often called **indirect speech**.
  Jo told Chris that there was nothing there except an old wooden box. (For more information, see Clauses pp. 63–66)

Interpersonal function

Mood

When we interact with others, we frame what we want to say as statements, questions or commands.
For example:
Aaron plays cricket for Queensland. (statement)
How many apples did you buy? (question)
Wait for me. (command)

Questions can be 'closed' (yes/no answer) or 'open' (require a longer answer).

Most of our interactions with others are concerned with exchanging and seeking information or negotiating goods and services. We therefore make different choices of mood, or grammatical structures that meet these needs.

Declarative mood – We make statements as we offer or exchange information. Such information may be statements of fact or may be the opinion of the speaker or writer.
For example:
We visited the National Art Gallery last Saturday. (fact)
The biggest problem for farmers is the lack of a permanent water supply. (opinion)

Interrogative mood – We ask questions to exchange information. Questions can be 'closed' (yes/no answer) or 'open' (require a longer answer).
For example:
Do you have enough money to buy a ticket? (closed)
Where did you go last week? (open)

Imperative mood – We command or request goods and services.

Fold the napkin in half.
Open the window, please.
Stand by for take-off.
Call the police!
Get out of here, now!
Empty your pockets.

Different grammatical moods predominate in different types of texts. Informational texts are largely written in declarative mood, while instructions and directions are largely given in imperative mood. In our day-to-day conversations, we move from one grammatical mood to another according to purpose.

(For more information, see Mood pp. 49-51)

Modality

When we interact with others, we often modify what we say, sometimes because we are uncertain, but mostly to be polite and get along with people. We achieve this through **modality** and **modulation**.

There is a group of words called **modals**, which we often add into our conversations and writings to show:

- **certainty** – how certain we are about something
- **usuality** – how often something happens
- **obligation** – how much obligation we impose on others

By doing this, we can make our intentions clear, but in a subtle way. Some examples:

Certainty	Usuality	Obligation
I will **definitely** come.	She **always** comes late.	You **must** stay here.
I will **probably** come.	She **often** comes late.	You **should** stay here.
I will **possibly** come.	She **sometimes** comes late.	You **ought** to stay here.
I **might** come.	She **seldom** comes late.	You **could** stay here.
Maybe I'll come.	She **never** comes late.	You **can** stay here.

We often modify the directness of our requests and suggestions by changing the wording of our messages. Between the directive to DO something and NOT DO something, there are a whole range of options we can choose. This is called **modulation**.

For example:
Get a haircut.
You must get a haircut.
You really should get a haircut.
It's time to get a haircut!
You could get a haircut.
You might like to get a haircut.
Why don't you get a haircut?
(For more information, see Auxiliary verbs p.26 and Adverbs p.42)

Get a haircut.

Attitude

Our interactions with others reflect our values, attitudes and emotions. We do this, almost unconsciously, through the words we choose to use.

For example: Instead of *strong* winds, we might use the more emotive *destructive, damaging* winds.

Speakers and writers create particular images of people and things through their choice of words. They often choose words specifically to give a positive or negative view of people, places, events and objects. Advertisers know this well, and choose those words that will present their products in the most desirable way. They use words like ***stunning, reliable, charming, immaculate, heavy-duty, the best deal ever, a once-in a-lifetime opportunity*** etc. Value can be ***outstanding, great, unbeatable*** etc. The media too, selects words designed to sway the audience to a particular viewpoint. It may choose words like ***murder*** or ***slaughter*** rather than ***kill***. Of a known terrorist, it may use words like ***evil, vicious, ruthless***, and his acts may be described as ***despicable, brutal*** or ***inhuman***.

TRY THIS

Compare these two reports. What are the attitudes shown by each reporter?

1 The prime minister told Parliament today that his party was studying the facts before making any decision on raising the incomes of pensioners.

2 The opposition demanded that the government take immediate action to substantially increase the income of the thousands of pensioners now living on the edge of poverty.

Textual function

Theme and rheme

The **theme** is the first part of a sentence. This focuses the reader or listener on how the text is unfolding. The **rheme** is the rest of the sentence.
For example:
Jillian (theme) finished reading her fashion magazine. (rheme)
She (theme) gave it to her sister to read. (rheme)
Her sister (theme) enjoyed reading it too. (rheme)

Throughout text, the themes form a pattern. This predictive patterning helps readers by establishing expectations of what will follow. This is an important aspect of planning and re-drafting your writing and ensures that texts will be understood.

Information text (typical pattern – Participant Process Circumstance)		
Theme	**Rheme**	
The Melanji tribe	lived	happily in the wild country of Cape York.
They	were	a peace-loving people.
They	hunted	for their food amongst the rocks and on the hot dusty plains.
The men	speared	emus and kangaroos.
They	caught	fish, turtles and crocodiles in the rivers and streams.
The women	collected	seeds, nuts and berries.

Note how the themes all relate back to the Melanji tribe, making the text cohesive and easily understood.
This patterning is typical of report writing.

Procedural text (typical pattern – Process Participant Circumstance)		
Theme	**Rheme**	
Beat	the butter and sugar	until smooth and creamy.
Add	the eggs	one at a time.
Add	syrup, pumpkin, mixed fruit, apricots and almonds.	
Stir		well.
Add	the flour	to the mixture.
Pour	the mixture	into a greased loaf tin.
Bake		at 180°C for 45 minutes.

Note how the processes take **theme** position. This is to make sure that what is important comes first.

Cohesion

Being understood depends on how clearly we articulate our thoughts and link our ideas together. This linking of ideas is called **cohesion**. These links are made by the use of **cohesive ties**. They tie parts of text together to create a unified piece of language.

Cohesive ties help writers and speakers to express the continuity of their ideas, and help readers to understand the meaning of a text. They can relate backwards and forwards, but can also refer to things outside the text in the known context.

Cohesion is created by reference, connectives, substitution and word choice.

Cohesion is achieved through:

❖ **Reference** (See p. 21)

Reference is a means of keeping track of the participants in a text. There are three forms of reference which establish meaningful links in text:

- **personal** (I, me, my, mine, you, your, yours, he, him, his, she, her, hers, it, its, we, us, our, ours, they, them, their, theirs)
- **demonstrative** (this, that, these, those, here, there)
- **comparative** (some examples – the same, other, similar, different, as big, bigger, equally, likewise, such, some, more)

This text illustrates the web of meaningful ties built up through reference. To what do these ties refer?

The day of the Maths Trail arrived. Our class felt very excited as our teacher, Mr Webb, divided us into small groups. He explained that the Trail was actually a series of maths activities. Some of them would be easier than others and points would be awarded for successfully completing them.

Chris, Sam and I were in one group. Armed with pencils and clipboards, we set off to Activity 6, which was our starting point. In this activity, we had to use a length of rope to work out the distance from the steps to the flag pole.

"This will be easy," said Chris. "Jayne, you are the tallest. We'll measure your height with the rope, then use this to measure the distance until we find out how far it is."
"I hope you know how tall you are!" exclaimed Sam.

❖ Connectives (See p.60)

Connectives are words and phrases that set up relationships between the ideas on either side of them. They relate one idea to another in a particular way.

We use them to show:

- **sequence of events** (first, secondly…lastly, then, afterwards, later)
- **cause and effect relationships** (therefore, however, although, because)
- **comparison and contrast** (alternatively, on the other hand, instead, whereas)
- **additional information** (also, furthermore, and, as well)
- **examples and results** (such as, for example, consequently, as a result)

These relationships are important in understanding what is being said, and for creating texts that are cohesive.

❖ Substitution

Substitution creates meaningful relationships in text by replacing one word for another. This avoids the need for constant repetition.

This text illustrates the web of meaning built up through substitution. To what do the highlighted words refer?

I am going to the supermarket to get a chicken for dinner. Do you want one?
I will probably also buy some bread and milk. Do you need any?
I don't know if you want any potatoes, but Jeremy would like some.

❖ Ellipsis

Ellipsis works in a similar way to substitution. Rather than use a substitute word, the word is left out altogether.
The author believes that the reader or listener can make the links to something previously stated, without the need for repetition.

I painted one wall and Tim painted the other (wall).
I won the first race, but not the second (race).
Jill does the shopping, Saul (does) the cooking and Doug (does) the cleaning.
Lynn liked the movie, but I didn't (like the movie).

❖ Word (lexical) choice

When we speak and write, we are constantly making choices about the **words** we will use. We choose words that go together, or are usually associated with each other in some way. These words form a 'string' or 'chain' of meaning as we build up a text about a particular subject.

These subject-specific words enable readers and listeners to keep track of the meaning. We repeat words and we use synonyms and antonyms.

We build meaning by constructing 'chains' of related ideas throughout text.

For example:

PAPUA NEW GUINEA

Papua New Guinea is situated just north of Australia, just below the equator.

Geography
Papua New Guinea is a rugged country and, until recently, some regions had never been visited by outsiders. A high range of mountains divides the country into north and south. There is no permanent road over these mountains, so people have to fly or walk from the north coast to the south. The valleys high in this mountain range are the most fertile.

Climate
The climate is generally hot and wet all year round. There are two seasons: the wet and the dry. Rainfall is very heavy. The capital, Port Moresby, is one of the driest parts of New Guinea with an annual rainfall of about 1000 millimetres. In the wettest part of the country, average rainfall is round 6000 millimetres. On the coast, the temperatures are similar all year: from 25 to 30°C. In the Highlands, it is much colder. On cold nights, ice will form on top of the highest summits.

Geography		Climate	
rugged	south coast	hot	average
regions	valleys	wet	rainfall
range of mountains	mountain range	seasons	temperatures
country	fertile	dry	centigrade
north	country	rainfall	degrees
south	Highlands	heavy	colder
mountains	summits	millimetres	cold
north coast		driest	ice
		wettest	

This text illustrates how word choices build whole-part relationships.

This reptile lived in Australia a long time ago. It does not exist now – but we know what it looked like because its bones have been found. It had a head like a crocodile, with rows of sharp teeth and a long thin neck. It had wings like a bat, although the bones of the hand were different from those of a bat. It had three fingers the same size, as well as a very long little finger. It had a light skeleton.

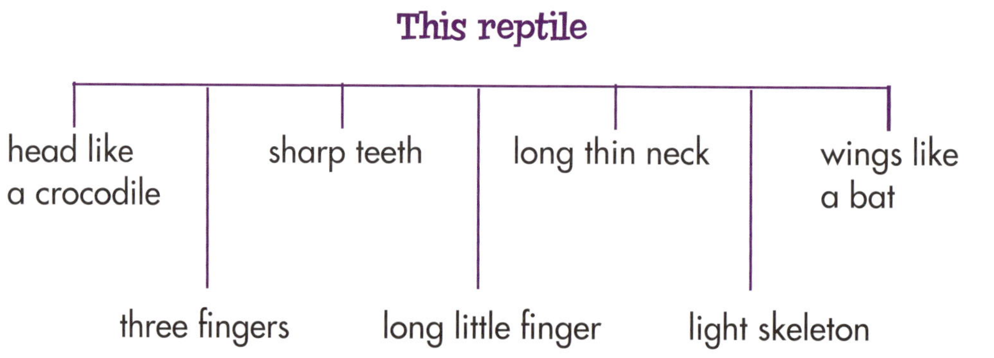

This text illustrates how word choices build class-member relationships.

Pasta is the general name for a range of nutritious foods made from a dough of wheat flour, salt, water and sometimes egg. There are many kinds of pasta including spaghetti, macaroni, vermicelli, tagliatelle, fettuccine and gnocchi.

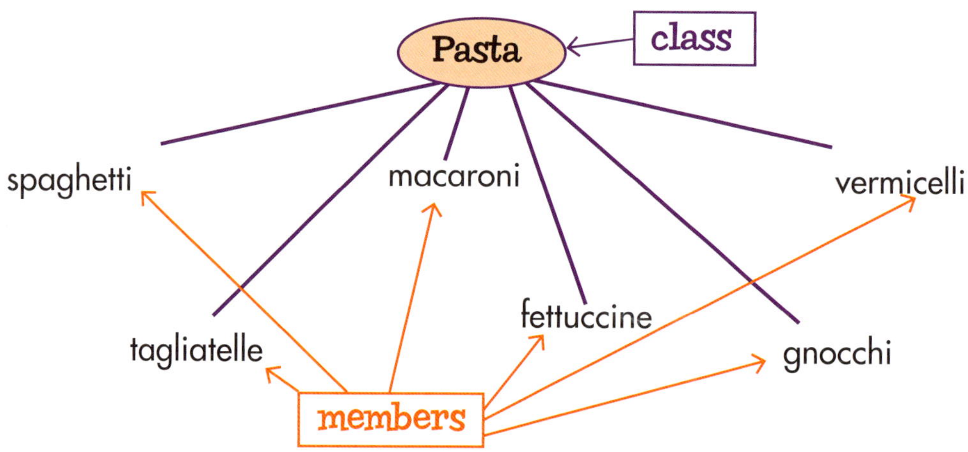

Circle the words that have been repeated in this text. Use different colours for different words.

Fred Wolseley came to Australia in 1854 and worked on a sheep station. Later, he bought his own sheep station in New South Wales. At that time, sheep were shorn with hand shears. Wolseley thought that shearing would be faster if shears were powered by a machine. He spent many years working on his idea and in 1884 he had invented the first machine shears. These shears could shear more quickly than hand shears. More wool could be cut in a day, and shearers could earn more money. In time, machine shears replaced hand shears altogether.

Voice

Verbs can be **active** or **passive**. A verb is **active** when its subject is doing the action.
For example: Rupert is playing the violin.

A verb is **passive** when the subject is NOT doing the action.
For example: The violin is being played by Rupert.

When we compose text, we often move between active and passive voice. This allows us to express our ideas in different ways, to put a different 'slant' on things. (See p.36)

William broke the window. (active voice)
The window was broken by William. (passive voice)
Most of the time, we use active voice in our exchanges. Passive voice makes our language more impersonal, and is often used in news reporting.

A verb is active when its subject is doing the action and passive when the subject is NOT doing the action.

Say whether these sentences are written in active or passive voice.

Storms have been predicted by the weather bureau. ________

Dingoes hunt and eat other bush animals. ________

Timber yards and warehouses are often guarded by fierce dogs. ________

The Spanish rulers of Cuba did not govern the island wisely. ________

A Christmas Carol was written by Charles Dickens. ________

Nominalisation

Nominalisation is the process of changing other word forms into nouns.
For example: loss from the verb lose
honesty from the adjective honest

This process allows us to make our texts more compact. We can give a lot of information in just a few words.

Examples:

1 A gymnast needs to be strong and control his body well while working on the rings. He needs to move his body smoothly and hold various positions without moving.

By using **nominalisation**, we can condense the information and 'tighten' the text to this:

- *Balance, strength and flexibility are the hallmarks of a great gymnast.*

2 Cane toads were introduced into Queensland in 1935 to combat cane beetles. The toads began to breed quickly and within six months their numbers had increased dramatically. Toads spread quickly into other areas as they continued to be released. However they did little to eradicate the beetles. An effective insecticidal spray was developed and cane farmers lost interest. Today cane toads inhabit large areas of land and have themselves become pests.

By using **nominalisation**, this text could read:

- *1935 marked the introduction of cane toads into Queensland to combat cane beetles. Their rapid breeding produced a dramatic increase in numbers. The release of more toads ensured their rapid spread to other areas. The eradication of cane beetles was only achieved through the introduction of an effective insecticidal spray. Today cane toads inhabit large areas of land and have themselves become pests.*

SELECTED ANSWERS

Page

4 Number nouns
plates, trucks, children, pencils, beaches, sheep, shoes, lunches, teeth, books, snowmen, violins

5 Compound nouns
fireplace, firelight, fireside, bushfire, riverbed, riverside, waterline, waterside, clothesline, headline, timeline, lifeline, underline, farmland, bushland, headland, underside, underwater, underclothes, farmhouse, lifetime, bedroom, headroom, waterway, underway, headway, headlight, hillside, topside

5 Collective nouns
crowd (of people), pod (of whales), shoal (of fish), school (of porpoises), flock (of birds), pod (of whales)

6 Abstract nouns
sorrow, glamour, hope, anger, tolerance, happiness, despair, grief

7 Verbal nouns
waiting, murmuring, screaming, cracking, roofing, whistling, whining

7 Gender nouns
aunt, uncle; goose, gander; stallion, mare; king, queen; gentlemen, ladies; ewe, ram; princess, prince; man, woman; rooster, hen

9 Noun groups
I, a cheeseburger, a piece (of) apple pie; a mean, sly fox; (around) the farmer's henhouse; (during) the night; rain; (on) rooftops (and) windowpanes; a family (of) noisy magpies; a shady tree (in) our garden; the class; an interesting documentary (about) earthquakes

12 Descriptive adjectives
sunny, cold day; new, red T-shirt; black shorts; trusty, old sneakers; fluoro laces; light breakfast; silver bike; school oval; fastest runner; finishing line; last place; great disappointment

13 Verbal adjectives
stewed, baked, amazing, cheering, fried, toasted, exciting, missing, howling, growing

Page

13 Adjective suffixes
comfortable, coastal, agreeable, foolish, personal

14 Antonyms
unhappy, unusual, untruthful, unclean, independent, informal, invisible, inappropriate, impossible, improbable, impatient, immature, illegal, illiterate, illegible, illogical

16 Adjectives of degree
faster, hottest, better, most, least, longest

16 Similes
quiet as a mouse; black as ink; straight as an arrow; shaking like jelly; pretty as a picture

18 Person
third, second, first, first, third

20 Indefinite pronouns
anyone (anybody, someone); everyone (everybody); none (nothing); any (some); someone (somebody, something)

21 Reference
She, his, He, She, her, he, he, it

23 Simple and compound verbs
Simple – fell, wait
Compound – is typing, is burning, will be leaving

24 Verb categories
shouted, enjoyed, screeched, wonder, will burn

25 Verb categories
is, has, is, are, have, were

27 Auxiliary verbs
You (could, should, must, will, can, did) wait for me.
Recycled water (may, might, will, could, can, should, would) solve the problem of water shortages.
Scientists (may, might, will, did, could) discover life on other planets.
He (may, might, will, did, has, could, must, would, should) not come.

Page

33 Regular verbs

Verb	I am …	Yesterday I…	I have …
cook	cooking	cooked	cooked
walk	walking	walked	walked
butter	buttering	buttered	buttered
shout	shouting	shouted	shouted
vote	voting	voted	voted
continue	continuing	continued	continued

34 Irregular verbs

Verb	I am …	Yesterday I	I have …
blow	blowing	blew	blown
begin	beginning	began	begun
lie	lying	lay	lain
write	write	wrote	written
ride	riding	rode	ridden
hurt	hurt	hurt	hurt
ring	ringing	rang	rung
break	breaking	broke	broken
shut	shutting	shut	shut
slide	sliding	slid	slid
know	knowing	knew	known
sing	singing	sang	sung
hit	hitting	hit	hit

39 Verb suffixes
criticise, falsify, flatten, classify, widen, sterilise

40 Adverbs of manner
silently, patiently, loudly, helpfully, quietly, coldly, clearly, badly, quickly, carelessly, noisily, recently

41 Adverbs of place
high, down, away, somewhere, here, nowhere, out, somewhere, off, behind, first, tenth

44 Antonyms
happily, then, loosely, well, low, loudly, outside, roughly, never, strongly, below, later

46 Participial phrases
- Standing waist deep in water, Sam signaled for help.
- Crowded with people, the bus set off down the dusty road.
- The students, dressed in school uniform, arrived at the museum.

Page

- Waiting for me was my father, holding a bunch of flowers.
- I just love pancakes, buttered thickly.

47 Adjectival phrases
cups, bell, box, chocolate, man

48 Noun phrases
- Riding skateboards is not allowed in the shopping mall.
- Smithy's dream was to fly solo across the Tasman Sea.
- Climbing Mt Everest was Sir Edmund Hilary's greatest achievement.
- We must learn to care for each other.
- Playing a musical instrument requires a lot of practice.

51 Mood
command, statement, question, command, exclamation

52 Subject
The hot air balloon; I; Golden autumn leaves; the go-kart; (You)

53 Object
Not every sentence has an object.
- no object
- direct object – tickets
- direct object – picnic lunch
- no object
- indirect object – Julie
- direct object – pair of skates; indirect object – him (Jack)

54 Compound sentences
Jess has an appointment at two o'clock, so she must leave early.
I would like to buy this jacket, but it is too expensive.
Would you like orange juice, or would you prefer lemonade?
I'm going to New Zealand and I would like you to come with me.

58 Indirect speech
Carol said that she had lost her earrings.
Mr Jack reported that the robber had escaped with a diamond necklace.
Anthony asked Patrick if he had read *The Water Horse*.
The teacher told the class to open their books at page six.

Page

65 Adverbial clauses
when, where, when, how, how long
Adjectival clauses
planet, person, invention, peaches, fossil

66 Noun clauses
- He pretended that he was asleep.
- You can tell that I've never done this before!
- That you lost your tennis match is hard to believe.
- I told the police I didn't know anyone by that name.
- Where I put my glasses is still a mystery.

70 Participants
The three, inexperienced schoolboys became lost in the rainforest. Many local people helped to search for them. They found the cold, hungry and frightened boys sixteen hours later.

The day of the Grand Final arrived. We entered the dressing rooms feeling both nervous and excited. After our warm-up and some final words from the captain, we jogged out onto the field. The crowd cheered and waved flags. Some of our supporters held banners and slogans. Some had painted their faces in our team's colours! We faced our opponents, full of excitement and confidence.

71 Processes
To earn some pocket money, David washes cars and cleans windows. 'doing'
We had been wondering where to go for our holidays. 'thinking'
What are you mumbling about? 'saying'
Philip will be sixteen next birthday. 'being'
A shark has razor-sharp teeth. 'having'

72 Attributes
Examples of possible attributes:
hot, strong, sweet, milky, black, white
warm, sunny, calm, winter, summer
hot, tired, hungry, busy
dry, dusty, empty, beautiful, green, inhospitable
favourite, faithful, pet, friendly, obedient

73 Attributes
The baby fox, feeling lost and lonely, huddled among the rocks.
The clown in baggy green trousers tumbled across the circus ring.
The letter from Aunt Emma was full of good news.
I bought a box of chocolates for my dad.
The man with the bald head stepped from the bus.

Page

79 Cohesion
The day of the Maths Trail arrived. Our class felt very excited as **our** (class) teacher, Mr Webb, divided **us** (class) into small groups. **He** (Mr Webb) explained that the Trail was actually a series of maths activities. **Some of them** (activities) would be easier than **others** (activities) and points would be awarded for successfully completing **them** (activities).

Chris, Sam and **I** (Jayne) were in one group. Armed with pencils and clipboards, **we** (Chris, Sam, Jayne) set off to Activity 6, which was **our** (Chris, Sam, Jayne) starting point. In this activity, **we** (Chris, Sam, Jayne) had to use a length of rope to work out the distance from the school steps to the flag pole.

"**This** (activity) will be easy," said Chris. "Jayne, **you** (Jayne) are the **tallest** (of Chris, Sam and Jayne). **We'll** (Chris, Sam, Jayne) measure **your** (Jayne) height with the rope, then use **this** (height) to measure the distance until **we** (Chris, Sam, Jayne) find out how far **it** (distance) is.
"**I** (Sam) hope **you** (Jayne) know how tall you (Jayne) are!" exclaimed Sam.

80 Substitution
I am going to the supermarket to get a chicken for dinner. Do you want one (chicken)?
I will probably also buy some bread and milk. Do you need any (bread and milk)? I don't know if you want any potatoes, but Jeremy would like some (potatoes).

83 Word choice
Fred Wolseley came to Australia in 1854 and worked on a sheep station. Later, he bought his own sheep station in New South Wales. At that time, sheep were shorn with hand shears. Wolseley thought that shearing would be faster if shears were powered by a machine. He spent many years working on his idea and in 1884 he had invented the first machine shears. These shears could shear more quickly than hand shears. More wool could be cut in a day, and shearers could earn more money. In time, machine shears replaced hand shears altogether.

83 Voice
passive, active, passive, active, passive

GLOSSARY

abstract noun	Noun which names a feeling or thought. *love, hope, despair, gratitude, anger, fear*
active voice	When a verb is active, the subject is doing the action. ***Rupert** is playing the violin.*
acronym	A word formed from the initial letters of other words. ***ANZAC** (**A**ustralian and **N**ew **Z**ealand **A**rmy **C**orps)*
adjectival clause	A dependent clause that says more about a noun in another clause. *The ladies, **who were all wearing purple hats,** enjoyed their trip to the theatre.*
adjectival phrase	A group of words that says more about a noun. *The girl **in the red dress.*** *A cup **of tea.***
adjective	Word used to describe a person, place or thing. ***hot** coffee; **tall** tree; **old** friend*
adjectives of degree	Three degrees – positive, comparative, superlative – which compare the qualities of people or things. *a **tall** boy, a **taller** boy, the **tallest** boy*
adverb	Word which adds to the meaning of the verb. It tells us how, when, where and for how long something is happening. *I moved house **yesterday**.* *She moved **quickly**. Put it **here** on the table. She trains **weekly**.*
adverbial clause	A dependent clause that adds information about the verb in the main clause. *You may all leave **when your desks are tidy**. I will wait **until it is done.***
adverbial phrase	A group of words that adds details about how, when, where, why or for how long something is happening. *I can hold my breath **for two minutes.** We went **to the park.***
adverbs of degree	Three degrees – positive, comparative, superlative – which show comparative differences in the time, place and manner in which things happen. *Liam arrived **early,** Sam arrived **earlier**, but Ned was **earliest** of all.*
agreement	Subject and verb agree in number. Singular subjects need a singular verb. Plural subjects need a plural verb. ***I am** celebrating. **We are** celebrating.*
antonyms	Words opposite in meaning to each other. *hot, cold; long, short; happy, unhappy*
apostrophe	A punctuation mark (') which shows: 1. ownership – *Chad's book; butterflies' wings* 2. where letters have been left out in contractions – *e'er, can't, didn't, it's*
articles	The words **a, an** and **the** used before a noun or noun group. ***The** cabbage. **The** queen. **A** boat. **An** egg. **An** hour.*
attitude	The choice of words we make reflects our values, attitudes and emotions.
attributes	Adjectives and adjectival phrases that add meaning to nouns. *a **sunny** day, the boy **in the blue cap.** The hikers, **feeling hungry and tired,** were glad to reach camp.*
auxiliary verbs	Words that are used in front of the verb to show future tense *(I **will** wait for you.)*; or in front of present and past participles. *(We **have** finished eating. They **are** waiting for a bus. She **has** written a book.)* Sometimes called 'helping' verbs.
base word	A word from which others are built. ***rest:** resting, rested, restful, restless, restlessly, unrest*
capital letters	Upper case letters used at the beginning of a sentence and for proper nouns (names), and in some acronyms. ***G**ive the ball to **J**acob. **W**e will watch the **O**lympic **G**ames on television.*
circumstances	Adverbs and adverbial phrases that tell us how, when, where, why and for how long something is happening. *Put the cup **on the sink.** Wait here **for five minutes.***

clause	A group of words with a subject and something to say about the subject.
clause complexes	Clauses joined together in various ways. Usually called 'sentences'.
cohesion	A linking of ideas within sentences and across text.
cohesive ties	Techniques for making text cohesive. See also **reference**, **ellipsis**, **substitution.**
collective noun	Name given to a group of animals, persons or things. *family, pack, mob, crowd, flock*
collocation	The process of choosing words that 'go together' so that an audience can quickly get the gist of what we are saying. ***car** – new, red, sporty, fuel economy, air bags, CD player*
common endings	Letters most often added to the ends of words. ***–ing** play**ing**; **-s** dog**s**; **-es** peach**es**; **-er** bigg**er**; **-est** bigg**est**; **-y** grass**y**; **-ly** sad**ly***
common gender	Nouns that are both male and female. *doctor, actor, artist, author, singer, friend*
common nouns	Names of everyday things. *coat, newspaper, shelf, pie, cupboard, chair*
complex sentence	Sentence consisting of a principal or main clause and any number of subordinate or dependent clauses. The clauses are linked by a conjunction or a relative pronoun. *When the bus arrived* (dependent clause), *only six people got off.* (main clause) *This is the house* (main clause) *that Jack built.* (dependent clause)
compound sentence	Sentence consisting of two or more principal clauses joined by **and, but, or, so** or **yet**. *I am leaving now, **so** you should lock the door. I'd like to go, **but** I haven't got enough money. Wash your hands **and** come **and** eat dinner.*
compound verb	Verb consisting of more than one word. *He **was playing** tennis. I **will be going** away.*
compound word	Two words joined together. *sea + shore = seashore; home + sick = homesick*
conjunctions	Words that join ideas together in a meaningful way. *Jack **and** Jill. It's getting dark, **so** I'll turn on the light. He was late **because** he lost his way. Wait **until** I call you.*
connectives	Words and phrases that link ideas together in certain ways. *He skinned his knees **because** he was not wearing knee pads.* (cause/effect) *He skinned his knees **and** made them bleed.* (result)
contraction	Shortened word or words. *I am – I'm; cannot – can't; it is – it's* An apostrophe marks the missing letters.
declarative mood	Language framed as statements. *I am going to the post office. Tim rides to school.*
definite article	The word **the**. ***The** prime minister of **the** country. All **the** eggs in **the** basket.*
demonstrative pronoun	Refers to specific people and things. ***this** program; **that** container; **these** children; **those** pictures*
dependent clause	A clause that says more about the main or principal clause and depends on that clause for its meaning. It is linked to the main clause by a conjunction or relative pronoun. *I go swimming **when the weather is hot**. I don't know the person **who lives here**.* May be called a subordinate clause.
direct object	Person or thing directly affected by the action of the verb. *I drank **the milk.***
direct speech	Sentences that record the speech of one person to another. Speech marks are required. *"I went to Darwin," said Finn. "Was it hot there?" asked Rhys.*
ellipsis	Cohesive tie. Words are left out by the author believing that the reader or listener can make the links without the need for repetition. *If you're buying **any**, get me **some** too.*
feminine gender	A group of nouns that name females only. *lady, girl, queen, hen, cow*

field	In language, refers to the things we want to talk or write about.
finite verb	Verb that has a subject. *Jake **walks** to school. Kerri **will visit** her cousins.*
'helping' verbs	See **auxiliary verbs**.
imperative mood	Language framed as command. *Sit up and listen. Wash your hair. Cut your hair.*
indefinite articles	The words **a** and **an**. ***An*** is used before a word beginning with a vowel or a silent 'h'. ***an** orange, **an** igloo, **an** honour*
indefinite pronoun	Refers to people and things in a general way. *few, many, some, everyone, nobody*
indirect object	Person or thing indirectly affected by the action of the verb. *I gave **him** the book.*
indirect speech	Speech reported by an onlooker or third person. *Katy told me that she was too excited to sleep.* 'that' is often omitted. *She said (that) I could come too.*
infinitive	Verb form, usually introduced by 'to'. *I like **to skate**. He wants **to build** a boat.*
intensifier	Adverb used to strengthen a message. ***extremely** fit, **very** old, **immensely** pleased*
interrogative adverb	Adverb used to ask a question. *How? When? Where? Why?*
interrogative mood	Language framed as question. *Have you seen Emily? Will you come back soon?*
interrogative pronoun	Pronoun used to ask a question. *Who? Whom? What? Which? Whose?*
intransitive verb	Verb with a subject but no object. *The explorers **sailed** away. The natives **cheered**.*
irregular verb	Past tense verbs and past participles that do not have the regular **-ed** ending. *blow, blew, has blown; break, broke, has broken; write, wrote, has written*
main clause	The main clause in a sentence. Can stand by itself. *Hannah cut a bunch of flowers.* Also called principal clause.
masculine gender	A group of nouns that name males only. *man, boy, prince, king, ram, rooster*
modality	Choices we make when we interact with others to show how certain we are of things, how often things happen, and how much obligation we are placing on them. We do this through modal adverbs and verbs. *might, should, must, definitely*
mode	In language, refers to the way we choose to exchange our messages with others. We most often do this through speaking and writing.
modifier	Adverb used to soften or weaken a message. ***rather** silly, **almost** ripe, **nearly** there*
modulation	Modifying the directness of our requests or demands on others by changing the wording of our messages. *Cook the dinner. Will you cook the dinner, please?*
mood	How speakers and writers frame what they say – as statements (declarative mood), questions (interrogative mood) and commands (imperative mood).
nominalisation	Process of changing other word forms into nouns. *pollute, pollution; lose, loss*
non-finite verbs	Verbs that need a 'helping' verb to make a complete verb. *Jake **is walking** to school.* Participles and infinitives are non-finite verbs.
noun	Word used to name a person, animal, place or thing. *man, mouse, park, cup*
noun clause	A dependent clause that works like a noun, and usually tells what someone is thinking, feeling or saying. *I had a feeling **that everyone was looking at me.*** It is often used in indirect speech. *Julian told me **that he had bought a dog.***

noun group	A group of words built around a noun. *an elephant; six, hot pies; some old clothes*
noun phrase	A group of words that works like a noun. Answers the question 'what'. ***Playing the piano** requires a lot of practice. **My favourite pastime** is riding my surfboard.*
object	Person or thing affected by the action of the verb, either directly *(I drank **the milk**)* or indirectly *(I gave **him** a book).*
paragraph	A number of sentences (usually less than 10) grouped around a single main idea. Paragraphs are usually separated by a double line space.
participants	The people, animals and things that are involved in the events we speak and write about. They are realised through pronouns and noun groups. *The steep hill, a plastic bucket, our class.* Participants are usually subjects or objects.
participle (past)	Word generally formed by adding **–ed** to the base verb. Used to show past tense *(I **walked** home)*; as verbal adjective *(**potted** plants)* and to begin phrases. *(The floods, **viewed** from the helicopter, **seemed** to cover the countryside.)*
participle (present)	Word formed by adding **–ing** to the base verb. Used to show continuous action *(I was **walking**)*; as verbal adjective *(**walking** stick)*; as verbal noun *(**Swimming** is good exercise.)* and to begin phrases. *(**Standing** on tip-toe, I saw...)*
passive voice	When a verb is passive, the subject is not doing the action. ***The violin** was played by Rupert.*
person	Refers to pronouns used to communicate: personally (1st person) to someone (2nd person) about someone or something (3rd person) 1st person pronouns – *I , me , my, mine, we, us, our, ours* 2nd person pronouns – *you, your, yours* 3rd person pronouns – *she, her, hers, he, him, his, it, its, they, them, their, theirs*
phrase	A group of words that add detail to sentences. They have no subject nor verb, so can only make sense within a sentence. *The man **in the straw hat** caught a fish.*
plural	Numbers more than one thing. Applied to nouns, pronouns and verbs. Plural nouns are formed by adding **–s** or **–es** to the singular noun. *cars, buses, peaches, dogs, boxes, cakes.* Some plural nouns are irregular. *child, children; mouse, mice*
possessive noun	Noun showing ownership. An apostrophe is used. *John's bike, all the dogs' bones*
possessive pronoun	Pronoun showing ownership. No apostrophe required. *my, mine, your, yours, his, her, hers, its, our, ours, your, yours, their, theirs*
predicate	The word or words that say something about the subject. *The boat* (subject) *was washed up on the beach after the storm* (predicate).
prefix	A syllable attached to the beginning of a word to change its meaning. ***un**happy, **dis**appear, **re**play*
preposition	Word used to position people and things. They often begin (prepositional) phrases. ***in** the park; **at** the movies; **under** the chair.* Their spelling never changes.
principal clause	The main clause in a sentence. Can stand on its own. *Hannah cut a bunch of flowers.* Also called main clause.
processes	Verbs (simple) and verb groups (compound) that tell us what is 'going on' in a text. There are 'doing', 'saying', 'thinking', 'feeling', 'being' and 'having' processes.

pronoun -personal (singular) -personal (plural) -in subject position -in object position	Word standing in place of a noun. They have singular, plural and possessive forms. *I, me, you, he, him, she, her, it* *we, us, you, they, them* *I, you, he, she, it, we, they* *me, you, him, her, us, them*
proper noun	The given name of people, places, objects and events. *Peter, Perth, Italy*
punctuation	A set of symbols used by writers to mark words, phrases, clauses and sentences so that readers gain meaning from text. Marks include: capital letters, full stops, exclamation and questions marks, commas, colons, semicolons, apostrophes, speech marks (or inverted commas), hyphens and dashes.
reference	Device used to keep track of the participants in text. Pronouns are used to refer backwards and forwards to a person or thing that has already been named. ***Jesse** got up early. **He** washed his face and got dressed. **He** made breakfast.*
regular verb	Verbs that can have 's', 'ing' and 'ed' added to them. *folds, bending, watched*
relative pronoun	Word used to connect one clause to another. The relative pronouns are *who, whom* (of people), *which, that* (of things). *There is the person **who** took our photo. Here is the clock **that** stopped.*
rheme	That part of the sentence that follows the **theme**.
rhetorical question	Question where an answer is not expected. *Can't come? That's disappointing.*
sentence	A meaningful unit of language complete in itself. *The spider spun a web. I feel well.*
simile	A phrase that shows the likeness between two things. *as cold as ice, as soft as silk*
simple sentence	Sentence consisting of one principal or main clause. *I drove to the coast on Sunday.*
simple verb	A verb consisting of one word. *They **ran** away. **Open** the door. I **wrote** a letter.*
singular	Numbers one thing. Applied to nouns, pronouns and verbs. *This **plane** is fast when **it flies.***
subject	Who or what a sentence is about. ***A lazy wind** stirred the leaves.*
subject/verb agreement	Subject and verb need always to agree in number. A singular subject has a singular verb. *The horse is eating oats.* A plural subject has a plural verb. *The horses are eating oats.*
subordinate clause	A clause that says more about the main or principal clause and depends on that clause for its meaning. It is linked to the main clause by a conjunction or relative pronoun. *I go swimming **when the weather is hot.** I don't know the person **who lives here**.* Also called a dependent clause.
substitution	A cohesive tie whereby one word is replaced by another. *Captain Cook arrived in his **ship**, The Endeavour. **This tiny vessel** was made of wood and was powered by the wind.*
suffix	A syllable attached to the end of a word to change the way the word is used. *great**ness*** (noun), *care**ful*** (adjective), *anxious**ly*** (adverb), *critic**ise*** (verb)
tag question	Question framed as a statement with a tag on the end. *You like pasta, don't you?*
tenor	In language, refers to the way we communicate with other people.

tense	In English we can show when events are happening: *are happening now* (present time); *have already happened* (past time) or *will happen* (future time). To show tense, we alter the verb. We can change the verb *(swim swam swum)*; we can add **-s**,**-ed** *(jump jumps jumped)*; use a helping verb *(will visit; shall see)* or use a helping verb with a participle *(is running; was skipping; have watched; had sailed).*
theme	The part we put first in a sentence to establish a pattern for the reader to follow. The theme is followed by the rest of the sentence, called the rheme.
transitive verb	Verb that passes the action from subject to object. ***The dog*** *caught the ball.*
verb	A word or words that tell us what is 'going on' in a sentence. *Jack* ***is picking*** *grapes. Ella* ***reads*** *books. Tom* ***rode*** *his bike to school. He* ***congratulated*** *the athlete.*
verbal adjective	Present and past participles used as adjectives. ***swimming*** *lessons;* ***dazed*** *expression*
verbal noun	Present participle used to name something. ***Skiing*** *and* ***skating*** *are winter sports.*

INDEX